Dear Dr. Wes…

Real Life Advice for Parents of Teens

Wes Crenshaw, PhD

With Teen Co-authors

Jenny Kane, Marissa Ballard Hemenway, John Murray,
Julia Davidson, Kelly Kelin Woods, Samantha Schwartz,
Ben Markley, and Miranda Davis

Based on the
Double Take Column
In the Lawrence Journal World

Publisher's Cataloging-in-Publication
(Provided by Quality Books, Inc.)

Crenshaw, Wes.
  Dear Dr. Wes : real life advice for parents of teens
/ Wes Crenshaw ; with teen co-authors Jenny Kane ...
[et al.].
  p. cm.
  Based on the Double take column in the Lawrence
journal world.
  LCCN 2011944953
  ISBN-13: 978-0615570402
  ISBN-10: 0615570402

  1. Parenting. 2. Teenagers. I. Kane, Jenny.
II. Title. III. Title: Lawrence journal-world.

HQ755.8.C74 2011   649'.125
                        QBI11-600225

Published in the United States of America by

www.familypsychpress.com

Also available on Kindle from Amazon.com

This is a great resource for parents. Buy it now and start reading—so that you'll have some ideas ready before problems hit. It would also make a fine gift for parents and kids on the cusp of teenageism. Imagine if they read the questions and discussed the answers together. Even if they didn't agree, (1) they'd be talking, and (2) they would be exchanging ideas and clarifying values about what is good and bad, right and wrong, healthy and not. It would be a Triple Take—Dr. Wes, his teenage column associates, and the readers! I recommend it wholeheartedly!

—**Michael Hoyt, PhD**, author of *Some Stories are Better than Others, The Present is a Gift, and Brief Psychotherapies;* and editor of *Therapist Stories of Inspiration, Passion and Renewal: What's Love Got to Do with it?;* and parent of a 24-year-old son.

I loved these two books—real questions from real people. One is for parents, needing answers as they navigate the rough waters of adolescence. The other for teens - those incredible, brilliant, energetic, maddening creatures leaping (often without looking) into adulthood, one foot lagging behind in childhood. The answers provided by Wes and the teen writers are always compassionate, always on everyone's side—thoughtful, blunt and sometimes raw in their honesty. These books should sit side by side on the shelf. Yes, there's one for parents and one for teens, but read BOTH! If you're a teen, you might see where your parents are coming from and how much they care. If you're a parent, you'll remember what you were like at fifteen, and more importantly, glimpse how challenging, how really challenging, it is these days to grow up healthy and happy.

— **Linda Daugherty** received the 2011 National Award from the Society for Adolescent Health and Medicine for her plays dealing with teen issues, *The Secret Life of Girls, Eat (It's Not About Food), dont u luv me?* and *hard 2 spel dad* (written with Mary Rohde Scudday). She has also been nominated by the Dallas Morning News arts staff for 2011 Dallas Morning News Texan of the Year. Her plays have been produced worldwide. She is playwright in residence at Dallas Children's Theater, named by Time Magazine as one of the top five theaters in the U.S. for families and youth, and a member of the Dramatists Guild of America.

DEDICATION

*To our readers who've
kept Double Take in the paper
and online every week since 2004.*

CONTENTS

All opinions and advice expressed herein belong solely to the authors and are not intended to substitute for psychological services. Readers are encouraged to seek professional guidance as necessary.

Email your questions on parenting teens to:

Ask@dr-wes.com

ACKNOWLEDGMENTS

Many thanks to the staff of the Family Therapy Institute Midwest for sponsoring the Double Take student scholarship from 2007 to 2010; and to Central National Bank for its additional funding. We owe a huge debt of gratitude to the Lawrence Journal World for giving ink to the only newspaper column on the planet that offers teenagers the chance to write advice to their parents and peers and for tolerating the controversies we sometimes create in the process.

Thanks also to Christine DeSmet, Faculty Associate at The University of Wisconsin-Madison for her ongoing consultation on the art and business of writing; Barrett Swanson, MFA for his keen editing and attention to the details of the English language; and the Kansas City Writers Group and e-Publishing Group for their support and encouragement of this project.

A final word of thanks to my mom, Marilyn Crenshaw, who finally got a chance to put her high school English award to the test as a proofreader; and to my daughter, Alyssa for her excruciatingly detailed read of the proofs.

Nothing you do for children is ever wasted. They seem not to notice us, hovering, averting our eyes, and they seldom offer thanks, but what we do for them is never wasted.

Garrison Keillor,
A Prairie Home Companion

1 DOUBLE TAKE

This is a book in which one board certified family psychologist[1] and eight really sharp teenagers offer candid advice to parents on just about every issue you may face with your adolescent: sex, love, contraception, pregnancy, sexual identity, school, divorce, self harm, the future, friendship, marriage (yours and theirs), college, suicide, anxiety, ADHD, hope and hopelessness, and so on. We also offer a healthy dose of social commentary, as we consider how the forces of our modern world are shaping the next generation—and vice versa.

If thinking about such things makes you squeamish, you may want to stop reading now. There are plenty of popular manuals in which childrearing experts offer something like, "Ten Days to Better Parenting in Seven Easy Steps." I'm actually writing one of those now, though I find it a bit like writing an operator's manual for software. Not one specific to Microsoft Word or Adobe Photoshop, just software in general. The problem is that while every computer program shares some common characteristics ("point and click the little icon of the disc"), each is more different than similar.

Such is the case with teenagers. One approach does not fit all. Each needs his or her own manual, the one you'll improvise and tailor to your kid for each unique situation. So, instead of offering a formula for parenting and hoping it fits, we'll get down into the trenches and

---

[1] I am a licensed psychologist and Board Certified in Couples and Family Psychology by the American Board of Professional Psychology.

troubleshoot some real questions asked by real teens and parents as they encounter real life.

Based on eight years of experience as an advice columnist, I know some readers will see our suggestions as quite liberal, particularly as they pertain to sexuality among teens. Others will see our advice as very traditional, emphasizing the importance of communicating values to teens, and treating one another ethically. However you choose to label our work, you don't have to agree with every word of it. In fact, you probably won't, and you'll find that sometimes even we don't agree with each other on the best approach to a given situation. That's why our column is called Double Take.

Instead, think of this book as *pragmatic*, coming from experience rather than theory, offering ideas and perspectives rather than rules and absolutes. It addresses the way things are for teens, not how we imagine or wish them to be. Like it or not, one decade into the millennium, these are the problems our teens face; the questions they ask adults—or worse, are afraid to ask. Their concerns run the gamut from excluding a friend from a sleepover to deciding when to have sex and with whom, to coping with unspeakable violence in the world around us. Our goal is to get parents and teens thinking and talking, as much as it is to suggest solutions to their specific problems.

No parents are merely interested in raising good teenagers. They're interested in raising good adults.

What makes this book and its companion for teenagers really unique, however, is the underlying concept of Double Take itself. Each week we write a column for the Lawrence Journal World that combines my nineteen years of psychological training and clinical experience with the youthful wisdom of a real expert on adolescence, a sixteen- to eighteen-year-old high school student selected each April from a pool of area seniors and exceptional juniors. The applicants submit essays and letters of reference, and attend an interview. A panel of writers rates their work on style, quality and substance.

The winner's "reward" is the chance to produce fifty columns a year handing out advice to their peers and parents, right out in the public eye, with no cute screen names to hide their identities. They also receive scholarship money for their freshman year at college, and each will get a share of royalties.

Roughly two thirds of these columns were written in response to letters submitted by teens and parents. The rest were written on topics the co-authors and I selected from current events, personal experiences, and trends affecting teens. Some were solicited from people who contacted me for clinical advice, though confidentiality and informed consent were carefully maintained. Some columns herein were updated and edited to minimize duplication and fit the format of a book.

Before we get started, I'll offer my first piece of advice: *Don't wait until you have a teenager to read this book.* If you're the parent of a younger child or preteen, now is the time to start your improvisation. If you digest this book cover-to-cover, you'll be ready for almost any parenting situation, and if something comes up that we didn't cover, send us an email and we'll get your question into the paper and online. If you've already passed the dreaded thirteen-year threshold with your child and feel like time is running out, don't worry. We've got you covered too. The chapter and column titles are laid out so you can browse and skim to pick out your *crisis de jour.* That way you can read fast, catch up and get ahead of the next curve. There will be many.

The original point of Double Take was to build empathy between generations and foster conversation on crucial issues. So, in that spirit of cross-training, we urge parents to read both volumes to get a better flavor of what your kids are dealing with and how best to advise them. Likewise, we urge teens to at least skim this book, even if they just want to know what we're whispering in your ear and see whether or not they agree with our advice.

Even as I was making final edits on both books, I found myself laughing on one page and near tears on the next. But, most of all, I was reminded of just how smart teenagers are, and how smart they have to be to get through this complex world we've created for them.

Dr. Wes and friends can't save your family from the therapist's office. In fact, we suggest therapy at least fifteen times in each volume. But we can help you know what to talk about if you end up there.

I'll close by offering my second piece of advice: *No parents are merely interested in raising good teenagers. They're interested in raising good adults.* We hope this book will offer a unique source of inspiration and guidance on that journey.

—Wes Crenshaw, PhD
ask@dr-wes.com

2 LOVE

Radical Monogamy

Dear Wes and Samantha,

My teenager is involved in a long-term relationship. I think she needs to be in less serious relationships at this point in her life and needs to date more than just one boy. What do you usually advise about this?

Dr. Wes: There are roughly two and a half dating styles among teens and young adults right now. Your daughter is in what I call the radical monogamy group. The other group engages in what is commonly referred to as "hooking up." Lacking a precise meaning—as most terms in modern coupling do—hooking up can mean anything from making out to having sexual intercourse, but it is by definition casual and recreational. I've no stats to prove it, but I'd say this is the norm at this point and I don't see that changing.

Needless to say, I'm not a fan. I've seen too many young adults who by age twenty-two are repulsed by their own teenage behavior, and for some it even wreaks havoc on their adult sexual satisfaction. I'm no prude, but I've yet to see anyone look back with joy on those years and remember fondly a long series of meaningless sexual encounters with random people they met at parties. Those who differ are free to write in.

Radical monogamy is more than a refurbished version of "going steady"—that quaint old tradition that had something to do with actually being a couple. The modern version is a little more militant, maybe even a reaction to casual sex.

These young people are defining themselves as exclusive boy- and girlfriends for years, beginning as early as seventh or eighth grade. Sometimes these are on-again, off-again, but they always seem to end up reconnecting.

Everyone needs to experience two dating behaviors as they grow up, exclusivity and exploration.

Halfway between hooking up and radical monogamy is another dating model referred to as "friends-with-benefits." Unfortunately, when you're having sex with a friend, you're begging for a bad outcome. The friendship is usually damaged and the absolute confusion that comes with having ill-defined boundaries and emotional bonds is difficult to avoid. Often, one friend pushes for a romantic relationship and the other resists, so the resulting power differential is usually hurtful and disappointing.

So, if I'm given a choice of options, I have to go with the one your daughter has selected. It's the closest analog for a healthy marital relationship later down the road. Yet, just as you propose, monogamy has shortcomings at this age. Locking in on one guy may limit an essential part of your daughter's developing identity. She may choose a partner at a very young age and then cling too tightly and for too long. That bond, enhanced by sexual intimacy, can push a relationship past its expiration date, making some radical monogamists emotional victims of their own healthy sexual boundaries.

My "rule" is this: Everyone needs to experience two dating behaviors as they grow up, exclusivity and exploration, in a reasonable balance. Your daughter favors one over the other, however, and getting her interested in "dating around" is really out of your control. You're better off just celebrating what she's trying to do and leaving yourself free to support and guide her when the nearly inevitable breakup occurs.

Samantha Schwartz: Although I understand you're concerned about your daughter's choice, there may be more to this story. If you saw the relationship as healthy, I have a feeling you wouldn't be writing us for advice. It's human nature to want to simplify a situation so it fits into a familiar mold and can be solved with a generic answer such as "long-term relationships are bad." However, you need to dig deeper and find out why you're so uncomfortable with her decision about this.

In your opinion, is the relationship emotionally and/or physically damaging? Does he insult her or make her feel guilty all the time? Does he constantly keep tabs on her, asking where she is or with whom? Does your daughter seem scared of him? If any of these seem true, have a talk with her immediately and help her get out of the relationship.

Beyond this, do you think their relationship is stunting the growth of their individual identities? Are they losing friends and isolating themselves? Talk to your daughter about qualities she likes about herself and what she wants to do with her life. Ask whether her friends ever feel left out because she's in a relationship and encourage her to hang out with people other than her boyfriend. Of course, most teenagers go through periods of being absorbed with one person. Learning how to balance her relationships may simply be a life lesson she has to learn right now.

If your daughter's health and safety are not at stake, try to accept her choice and not be too nit-picky about her boyfriend. He may be her perfect match or just another guy she dates. It doesn't matter. Having a serious relationship teaches her important lessons about meeting another's needs without sacrificing her own, respecting another's boundaries, and working through disagreements. Being monogamous at this age doesn't come with a tag that says "right" or "wrong." It all depends on the nature of the relationship.

Older Guy

Dear Dr. Wes and Samantha,

I'm having a hard time knowing how to handle my daughter's relationship. She is sixteen and wants to date a man who is twenty-one. I think there is something wrong with this. I don't know why he would be interested in a girl this young.

Samantha Schwartz: A younger girl dating an older guy comes with assumptions: he's pressuring her to have sex; he likes having control over her; he will introduce her to drugs and alcohol prematurely. However, these stereotypes may not apply here. Your daughter may be ready to date a guy who is more mature than her peers or maybe she just has more in common with him than she does with guys her age. Either way, this relationship could be good for her.

While there is evidence that girls dating older guys are more likely to face relationship violence and to abuse substances, relationships are not statistics. It would be a mistake to forbid your daughter from dating him just because you think dating an older guy is "risky." That would be like throwing away an apple because there *might* be a worm in it. Besides, your insistence probably won't stop her and may actually make her more attached to him.

If you want to protect your daughter, you need to approach the situation differently. Invite the guy over for dinner. Don't pull out your shotgun or start an interrogation. One open-ended question goes farther than a hundred closed ones. Find out what activities he's involved in and show a genuine interest in at least one. Ask him follow-up questions about that activity. Find out what he's proud of, and what's difficult for him.

Google him. You probably won't find much information on a college student, but you never know. If your daughter talks to him on Facebook, casually look at his profile while she's online. It can reveal a lot about a person. If he lives in the community, ask about him.

In getting to know him, your daughter is your best source. Ask her why she likes this guy. Show respect for her decision through your interest in her thoughts about him. Once you show you're on her side, she'll be more open to your questions. Ask her about her sexual boundaries, and if he's pressured her in any way. When she goes out on a date with him, find out the details of their plan. Then follow up to see how it went.

Frequent dialogue is important whether your daughter is dating someone her own age or someone older. Your best option is to stay connected with her. A shared interest in her happiness will strengthen your relationship so that, if and when she determines she is in over her head, she will come to you.

Dr. Wes: I have one simple rule on this subject: The older they are the more perfect they have to be. It's one thing for your daughter to date unwisely when her partner is an age mate. When the difference is five years, two important factors have to be in sync. First, the guy needs to be interested in her because she is a remarkably mature young woman. The worst thing I ever hear in these cases is a girl who gleefully declares, "Don't worry, he doesn't act like he's twenty-one!" Somehow that's supposed to equal things out—the guy is so childlike that he fits perfectly into the sophomore class.

Instead what you want to see and hear is that your daughter is so sophisticated that, just as Samantha proposes, she actually fits in better with the college age crowd. That's hard to gauge, but you have to figure it out before knowing what's going on with this guy. Truth be known, I've advised more than one seventeen-year-old who was too emotionally mature for high school to look for dating partners aged nineteen or twenty. You just have to stick to the rule if you want it to come out okay.

Second, the guy has to be near-perfect in a lot of other ways too. He'd better be working consistently in a decent job or doing well in college or trade school, and have some ambition for the future. Again, those things don't matter as much if he's a teenage boy. They count for everything in a young adult.

After you've followed all of Sam's excellent suggestions and determined that this guy is okay, sit down and get the big issues out on the table. Young adults have easy access to a great many things that teenagers should not. Your daughter must keep following house rules (curfew, grades, etc.) and her boyfriend needs to support that *without fail*. He should be especially aware that he faces serious charges if he's furnishing her with legal or illegal substances. Again, teens tend to be careless about some of these issues. Adults had better not be. If he can support and follow your limits, you may find that this guy is actually a safer bet than some of your daughter's peers, who have all the same problems you fear and less maturity. If your daughter wants to play in his league, she needs to play smart.

One last thing. None of this advice applies to relationships that are criminalized by law, and anyone dating in this age range needs to understand the age of consent in his or her state, usually sixteen, seventeen or eighteen. It is extraordinarily easy for older teens and young adults to end up as sex offenders before realizing they've crossed a legal line, and courts aren't taking those cases lightly. Unless you've studied this more closely than the average citizen, you've no idea how damaging it will be for a son or daughter who gets caught up with an underage partner. It can destroy one's future in about ninety seconds.

Older Woman

Dear Dr. Wes and John,

I saw your article about underage dating[2]. I have a similar situation. My son is not quite seventeen and is in love with a twenty one-year-old woman who is over four years older than him. They met at a job where he no longer works. She started confiding in him that she'd been sexually harassed at the current job and at a past one. She also took a trip to another country where she was supposedly drugged and sexually mistreated. She's never reported any of this. Neither of them see anything wrong with their relationship, but I have done my best to stop them. We recently learned they were sneaking around behind our backs and we've taken some more drastic measures. Am I out of line? I want my son to lead a healthy and normal life, and I can't see that happening with someone like this around. I see her as a pedophile and it makes me ill to think about it.

John Murray: Captain Obvious once said that teenagers like to be rebellious. You can tell your son to invest his hard earned money, but that may convince him to blow it on the slot machines. This "girlfriend" has made herself out to be flashier than Las Vegas and your son thinks he's won the jackpot. Every day he pours his time, money, and credibility into this casino of a woman, thinking he can beat the dealer and win it all. Your haughty disapproval and this woman's tabloid background only add to the thrill of the game.

Slot machines have warning signs, but that does little to deter hardcore gamblers. Your son knows the risks he's taking. He just chooses to ignore them. An emotional tirade won't convince him to fold, because it is partly your frustration that has encouraged him to go all in. Instead, keep your cards close to your chest. Try to avoid talking about this woman, and don't raise your voice when the subject comes up, but when he asks for your approval, tell him "no dice." Start adding little restrictions here and there, slowly tightening the noose around his social life. If you threaten him now, your son will think you're bluffing. But if

---

[2] This column is found in Chapter 3 of *Dear Dr. Wes...Real Life Advice for Teens*, under the title "Age Inappropriate."

you're calm and consistent with your consequences, he'll know you play to win.

Reality will kick in soon enough. This woman is obviously taking advantage of your son and I'll give eleven-to-one odds this "relationship" will end reeling in heartache. So make sure you're understanding and don't push the "I told you so." Once your son has come to realize his mistakes on his own, he'll be more eager to cover his losses. When that happens, it's time for some discussion, professional therapy, and adjustment to life as usual.

Your son is lucky to have a wise parent taking care of him, which is a good deal more than I can say for his "girlfriend."

Dr. Wes: You raise some deeply concerning issues, but they're less about age and more about the mismatch in experience this woman brings to the relationship. I am particularly concerned about her introduction of sexually laden material—especially involving her own sexual abuse—to a sixteen-year-old. Additionally, given developmental differences between genders, a woman of twenty-one showing interest in a teenager makes her suspect in my book. She's obviously very immature, which doesn't help matters a bit.

You don't have to tell your son that you approve of this, but the more you fight it the more interesting it will become.

That said, there are some serious limits on what you can really influence here with an almost seventeen-year-old. We see this more commonly with the genders reversed and it's nearly impossible to pry those relationships apart. Technically, you have a right to try, but practically, you're guaranteed to drive them closer together as they defend their unique and magical love from the onslaught of inconsiderate authoritarians who've forgotten what real romance is—or something equally melodramatic.

The big difference between this situation and the column you cite is that your son is over the age of consent in this state and a year short of adulthood himself. While it may be distasteful to you, it certainly is not pedophilia. A pedophile is a person who is sexually interested in prepubescent children, not a very young adult who likes to date teenagers. That may seem far too fine a distinction, but it is critical. Your son is acting normally by being attracted to an interesting, provocative "older" woman. The fact that she brings in some odd baggage probably makes the thrill even greater.

John's poker-faced position is tenable, but we differ on how much pressure you can bring to bear on your son. Years ago I presented an even ickier scenario (seventeen-year-old girl, thirty four-year-old ex-convict) to my mentor. She told me that instead of lecturing this client about how awful her situation was, I should invite this dude to therapy and treat the situation just as seriously as the girl did. I did exactly that and he was history in a few days. It won't be that quick for you, but it's always best to keep your friends close and your enemies closer. You don't have to tell your son that you approve of this, but the more you fight it the more interesting it will become.

Engaged at Eighteen

Dear Dr. Wes and Samantha,

Help! My daughter topped off graduation with an announcement that she and her boyfriend are engaged and want to get married before they go to college. There is no pregnancy and in my mind no reason for her to be getting married so they can live together. What can I say to stop them? We like her boyfriend and think of him as a member of the family, but the statistics on young marriage are terrible. We think they are destroying all the good things in their lives by taking this step right now.

Samantha Schwartz: In *When Harry Met Sally*, Harry says, "When you realize you want to spend the rest of your life with somebody, you want the rest of your life to start as soon as possible." While Harry may be right, you'll want to remind your daughter that the rest of her life doesn't have to begin with marriage and living together.

Because she is an adult, however, you can only reason with her. Have a discussion with her alone when she is in a calm mood and ask her to think over a few things before taking these monumental steps. Tell her how much you like her boyfriend and that you would be happy to see them married in the future, so it's clear your feelings have nothing to do with him or their relationship.

Be understanding. Explain to her that coming to college married won't necessarily destroy her life, but it could be detrimental to her freshman experience. As someone with a serious boyfriend for two and a half years, I know what it's like to be thought of as one unit. We're attending the same college, and this perception will be even more prevalent as we meet new people. We've discussed the importance of introducing ourselves as separate people with individual identities. Your daughter needs to realize that being married and living with him at college will make her seem unapproachable and not relatable to other college students. College is not just about academics; it's about meeting people with new points of view and learning about oneself as a person.

Ask her to give this decision some time. Tell her you would prefer that she give unmarried college life a chance, at least during their first year. Let her know that you just want her to be happy, and you don't want her to miss out on a once-in-a-lifetime experience.

Dr. Wes: You're right to be concerned, though you're just as power-less as Samantha proposes. While we all know couples that met in high school and are still together twenty-five or fifty years later, those statistics you mention don't lie. Early marriage is an astounding predictor of marital failure. In fact, every birthday you add on before marriage up to age twenty-seven increases the couple's chances of staying married. So the best argument for your daughter not marrying at eighteen or nineteen is to preserve the long-term hopes for the relationship.

Rooming with anyone is a trying experience, especially a romantic partner, and especially in the late teens and early adult years.

Having been at this for about as long as your daughter's been alive, I've grown frustrated with the way we approach love in our society. We lift up and magnify every aspect of mating that's likely to fade with time—like super-double, earth-shattering romance and mind-blowing sex—and downplay all the ones that actually predict marital success, like stability, emotional maturity, shared values, and good-matching.

There's a good reason for this. Very few romance novels or movies would sell if their tagline read: "He was a mature young man. She was an emotionally stable young woman who shared his vision for the future. Together they formed a solid and cohesive family unit that was the envy of their friends, and retired quietly in Boca Raton." Snore, snore. We all want explosive drama and wild romantic twists to entertain us. Except none of us are actually in those movies and they end before we ever find out how things really turned out. So we've no idea whether Romeo and Juliet would have been a happily married couple, or if the *Titanic* kids would have still been together seventy years later.

If we can't rely on that narrative of love to guide young people in marrying, what can we rely on? Growing up. That's the simple wisdom in the advice you're trying to give your daughter. You're not asking her to scorn her true love in favor of a Capulet. You're just asking her to give her relationship the best shot, and by any measure that means waiting for adulthood before taking the plunge. It's also good to remember that all relationships are four-dimensional, meaning they exist across time. One can only get a sense of the future by waiting to see how some of it turns out.

I couldn't tell why from your letter, but for some reason your daughter and future son-in-law think they have to marry to live together. That's a neat tradition, but pressing it will only force early marriage. If I were you, I'd take the heat off that topic. You like this guy, so don't discourage the couple from living together for a few years. Unfortunately, statistics also tell us that while most currently-married couples lived together before marriage, the vast majority of live-in romances end without marriage. Rooming with anyone is a trying experience, especially a romantic partner, and especially in the late teens and early adult years. So they should move cautiously even on cohabitation, and thereby increase the likelihood of ending up retired together in Boca.

It beats ending up alongside the majority of Americans whose marriages fail.

Boyfriend Home for the Holidays

Dear Dr. Wes and Kelly,

My daughter just turned twenty, but I hope you'll still answer this because it's also a problem for parents with teens and you've written about it from the child's perspective before[3]. She's coming home for Christmas break and wants to bring her boyfriend. She goes to a distant college, so she's only home once a year. She went with him for Thanks-

---

[3] One such column is found in Chapter 10 of *Dear Dr. Wes...Real Life Advice for Teens*, under the heading "Home for the Holidays."

giving and usually goes with friends on spring break. She may not even come home for the summer because she has a job in her college town that she doesn't want to leave because of the economy. We feel like this is our only chance to see her and we want to focus our time on family. We don't dislike her boyfriend; we just feel kind of invaded—and we're worried about having a big drama over sleeping arrangements. Is it too much to expect her to reserve some time for us once a year?

Dr. Wes: This is one of those perennial problems that has at least "two hands," one where you stick to your guns to preserve family tradition and the other where you flex to meet changes in your daughter's life. Consider the risks and benefits of each before deciding. By my calculation, your daughter is spending less than 10% of her time in her family home at this point. That's probably about average or a little less for her age. So it's understandable that you would miss her and want to cherish the opportunities you do have for family time. Given that she has the other 90% of her time to spend in her world of school, friends, work and romance, I agree that you're not asking too much for her to give you most of her Christmas break. As a reasonable compromise, you might offer to host the boyfriend for a full week in late December and/or early January. Maybe even pay his flight out and back, if that's affordable. In exchange, she'll give you the Christmas week for family time. If you provide enough enthusiasm for his visit, she may see your side of things.

I know you're worried that your daughter is drifting away, but her establishment of an adult identity is a fact of life.

I'm always a big advocate for families understanding the developmental milestones of their late-teenage children and helping them successfully leave home. There's no higher calling in a family than to help launch children toward a life of independence. But I also encourage teens to have some empathy for their families as they work their way through that same process. Likewise, after their mid-twenties, many folks look back with regret on how little time they spent with family.

Your daughter seems to be doing just fine on her own and you should be proud of her. Now is a good time for her to begin considering her independent self in a larger, interdependent context. Part of that involves negotiating something that meets your needs as well as hers.

Similarly, it's reasonable for you to ask her not to sleep with her b.f. while visiting your home, but be cautious about how many other rules you put in place beyond that. Parents should pick their battles with teens wisely to avoid unnecessary conflict, especially if they want the holidays to yield family harmony.

Kelly Kelin[4]: Home for the holidays can be stressful enough with last minute shopping and gift wrapping and cooking big family dinners, let alone the added stress of your daughter's boyfriend coming along. You've raised your daughter all these years, helped her along the way, and now you rarely see her. You may feel cheated. However, your daughter is in a different stage in her life, establishing herself as an adult and slowly migrating away from you. How you handle this situation will influence where she wants to go for this and future holidays. Look at it from her perspective. She went to the boyfriend's parent's house for Thanksgiving and now she wants to bring him home for Christmas.

If you choose to allow the boyfriend to come to your home, make sure you enforce your rules. If you don't feel comfortable with them sleeping in the same room, then insist on other arrangements. They should respect this decision. After all, this is your house. Just be careful not to make that enforcement seem hostile.

If you're worried you won't have any time with your daughter, make time. Perhaps your husband can take the boyfriend off your hands while you and your daughter go shopping or make dinner together. Then you and your husband can switch roles so both of you can spend time with your daughter. This would also give you an opportunity to learn more about her boyfriend.

I know you're worried that your daughter is drifting away, but her establishment of an adult identity is a fact of life. She is an adult now and can choose not to come home at all. Would you want a Christmas where you and your husband will be alone?

Think it through before you make your decision.

---

[4] Kelly changed her last name to Woods after completing her tenure on Double Take. Her column byline remains Kelin, her name at the time they were written. She is however, listed as Kelly Kelin Woods for the authorship of this book.

Obsessive Love

Dr. Wes: When working with teenagers I often propose that most relationships through the mid-twenties are practice for the longer-term loves that lie ahead. I'm not diminishing the importance of those experiences. Quite the opposite in fact. They form the foundation for how emerging adults choose to treat themselves and their future partners. With adult clients, I can often trace the roots of dysfunctional sexual and romantic habits all the way back to junior high and high school. There's an old saying, you go from where you start, and nowhere is this truer than in romance.

It follows that if teens start off in emotionally or physically abusive relationships, they may habituate to those same circumstances over time. In other words, if what you practice is accepting the mistreatment of others, then that is what you will become good at. And sadly, it doesn't take much for that pattern to take hold and a lot to disrupt it.

All this intensity and obsession may seem very romantic in the movies, but in real life it has another name—stalking.

We understand that if a son or daughter comes home with a black eye or bruised arm from a partner, that's abuse and it should be pursued as a domestic battery complaint. What's less obvious and thus more insidious is emotional damage inflicted between teenage partners. Parents need to understand their teenager's dating practices, beliefs, values, and struggles, simply to look out for their interests. Many are having a hard time with their love lives, whether they recognize it or not—some as victims, some as offenders and some as a complex mix of both.

The most recent installment of this problem is what I call the "obsessed breakup" and it borders on the abusive. It used to be that teenagers broke up, hated each other, and moved on to other partners while the world kept spinning. Now they need more remedial work on how to end a relationship than on how to start one. The old breakup line "we can still be friends" used to be a nice way to say, "kiss off." Now teens really mean it, and they move back and forth between friends and lovers in a chaotically intense pattern that maximizes jealousy, hurt feelings, and a general stuckness.

Routinely I hear that Bobbi Sue and Billy Joe broke up, then Billy Joe threatened to "kick the butt" (so to speak) of any guy who wants to be with Bobbi Sue, even if *he* did the breaking up. Sometimes these threats are serious and really do lead to violence. The exact same ethos has emerged for girls too, and sometimes it's even worse. Bobbi Sue is just as prone to send "her girls" after Billy Joe's new love, even if she unceremoniously dumped him.

Parents should understand that young people don't have this all figured out just yet and, at times, may need your help. While ill-considered limits on dating beg a Romeo and Juliet romance, an obsessive or abusive relationship is one of the few good reasons to intercede. When that situation arises, parents need to issue only one demand: Stop the madness.

While dating at this age is important, nothing is *this* important. Nobody needs to be obsessed with anyone, especially at sixteen. Few experiences in adolescence constitute the end of the world, but instead mark the beginning. So, help your kids start out right. All this intensity and obsession may seem very romantic in the movies, but in real life it has another name—stalking.

Kelly Kelin: I strongly believe that the seriousness of relationships in high schools is overrated. Teens too often throw around the "love" word without ever recognizing its true value and meaning. Teens may believe their relationship will last forever with a fairy tale ending, but the chances of that actually happening are unlikely. Yes, I may not be much of a romantic, but it's time to wake up and be realistic about things.

Teen relationships can quickly sour, and teens in abusive relationships are often too deluded to acknowledge obvious warning signs. They may be dependent personality types, basing their own value of themselves on others' perceptions. The abuser in the relationship will take advantage of this, taking a position of power by acting manipulative, controlling, and emotionally or physically abusive.

As a parent, it may be hard to recognize whether or not abuse is happening to your child. When discussing your suspicions, be sure to remain open to his or her views. However, several warning signs may become apparent. There may be changes in your child's mood and behavior, such as withdrawal from the family. The partner may have anger issues, show signs of too much jealousy, or shift blame for every problem on your child. Your child may be oblivious to this problem, so if you become aware of any abuse, take immediate action.

Marissa's Wedding

Dr. Wes: This week's column went safely to bed just as my weekly life-altering experience reached out to grab me. It arrived in the form of a wedding. I didn't see it coming because, frankly, I'm not a big fan of weddings. Long time readers know I'm a big romantic. Heck, I helped Samantha's boyfriend ask her to prom this year, and wrote about my impromptu interview at Chili's of two high school kids in love[5]. So what's not to like about weddings, and how does that fit into a column for parents of teens? In my view, young couples in their overabundance of romance and shortage of forethought, put more time, energy and planning into their thirty-minute ceremony than they do their lifetime of marriage. Wouldn't it be wiser to stow that money in a savings account and take a lifetime of honeymoons, symbolically renewing their vows year after year?

Each day you get up and decide to be married again, not just when it's easy and beautiful and fun, but when it's hard and ugly, and it sucks.

So I went to this wedding not for a heartfelt moment of sheer joy, but because the bride was Marissa Ballard, Double Take columnist from 2005 to 2006. Marissa also helped conceptualize the column and helped judge the contest every year until 2010. Beyond that, she's one of my favorite young people and we've stayed in touch ever since she left for Pittsburg State University.

In terms of gifting, I never go with the bridal registry. My wedding gift keeps on giving—John Gottman's book *The Seven Principles for Making Marriage Work*. You'll find it at the bookstore on a shelf labeled Marriage and Divorce. No, seriously. Nowadays, booksellers mix up the titles on marriage with those on divorce and child custody. That way you can pick up both in one trip, so you're ready if the marriage fails, which, statistics tell us, it probably will.

---

[5] Both of these sweet columns appear in Chapter 2 of *Dear Dr. Wes...Real Life Advice for Teens.*

Life fools me again. Over 48 years, I've been to many weddings, but none more moving than Marissa's. Rather than a lot of pageantry and pomp, I saw two young people surrounded by friends and family in a simple setting, overwhelmed by their emotion for each other. I won't invade the sanctity of the moment by giving a play-by-play, but the sense of love and togetherness between the couple made it feel as if the rest of us had disappeared into the background, leaving them alone, together perfectly, as they shared their promises. Then, they turned and rejoined us, the community. I've never clapped so hard at a wedding. It touched my heart and made me want to go home and be married another 25 years, which I shall now do.

That brings us to the point of this column, short and sweet. Many young people today do not trust the "us" of the world. As teens they see too much divorce and destructive sexual behavior amongst adults. We like to think they're getting that unhealthy diet from TV or the Internet. Don't kid yourself. It's closer than that. In turn, they form transient relationships, relying far too much on the recreation of sex and too little on its spiritual essence. Teenagers instead need role models who show them that getting married is not about your wedding day—no matter how deeply moving it may be. It's about the next day and the one after that, and a lifetime of those days. Each day you get up and decide to be married again, not just when it's easy and beautiful and fun, but when it's hard and ugly, and it sucks. You fight for the relationship not because you don't want to end up divorced, but because you want to end up married.

My deepest congratulations to Marissa and her new husband, Arna Hemenway, as they take the journey together, and to all the young couples who follow them. Marry well, trust the "us," and fight for it.

Samantha Schwartz: I haven't been to many weddings yet. I've attended a couple of traditional white ones, with a bride donning a lovely dress, flower girls sprinkling petals down the aisle, and a ballroom reception. Like Wes, those things never moved me. The most beautiful ceremony I ever attended was anything but traditional. My godparents' wedding, a humble backyard affair; the wedding party dressed in shorts. During the ceremony, we sat on a canvas painter's cloth laid across the grass.

The wedding couple was my godparents, and other than my own parents, they're the greatest example of a loving relationship I've had the honor to witness. They enjoy each other's company every day; my sister says they always seem to be on their honeymoon. Between the two of them, they can do anything. Ranae excels at woodworking, line dancing, and teaching, and Jan is a fantastic singer/songwriter and an expert at web accessibility for people with disabilities. They support each other's interests, offering one another help even while juggling fifteen other projects. It's fun to watch them brainstorm together; they encourage and inspire each other to achieve great things. Every day, Ranae makes Jan a blended ice mocha, which Jan greets with a dazzlingly gracious smile. I want to have a marriage like that. One where the little things count.

At their small wedding, each of us shared a story, speech or poem, something wonderful about Jan and Ranae's relationship. When they read the vows they'd written for each other, they were both in tears, along with the rest of the guests. Jan and Ranae have never been bored with each other or strayed from their commitment. They're the light in each other's lives, the reason each gets up every morning to face another day.

They'd been together over fifteen years before their wedding day. It came during the small window of time in which gay marriage was legal in California. It's astonishing to me that a couple of this caliber could not be married in most states; they have a better marriage than ninety-five percent of the couples I know.

In fact, everyone has something to learn about love from Jan and Ranae.

3 SEX

The Talk

Dr. Wes: I recently heard a delightful story on youth radio (youthradio.org) by Johanna Greensberg, a teen commentator from Blunt radio in Maine. She opens, "I'm sorry to say this, but parents are falling down on the job when it comes to 'the talk…' When we compare notes, my friends and I realize we are learning about sex from the Internet and the movies because our parents aren't talking with us." Then Johanna asks her mother why she didn't talk to her about sex. Her mom says, "I think that I did." Johanna insists that she did not, and when pressed, her mom can only remember saying, "I hope you wait…" then she adds, "or maybe that was with somebody else."

I couldn't suppress a laugh.

Johanna's style was so wry and biting, like the Borat of teenage girls going around asking, in a humorous in-your-face kind of way, really uncomfortable questions that every

> It's never too early to begin having The Talk. The sooner you start, the more comfortable both of you will be as your child ages and you become more practiced.

parent should be considering but aren't. At one point, she presses her dad for The Talk. He stammers, "I would like you to know that sex is a part of love and a part of a relationship and it's a part of a way that you show caring in a relationship…the other part is, of course, the consequences of you know...pregnancy, HIV, and those...are the kind of...did I say pregnancy?"

I almost pulled over to the side of the road.

Chuckles aside, Johanna was hitting a serious point I hadn't considered recently. In my job, teen sexuality is about as uncomfortable as a flat tire is for a mechanic—all in a day's work. Johanna's commentary reminded me how tough and scary sexuality is for many parents, like the girl she interviewed whose sex talk involved her dad telling her to pay attention when a condom ad came on TV.

Johanna suggests several ways to make The Talk go smoother. First, don't assume kids know anything—cover all the bases. I'm still mortified at teens who honestly believe one cannot get pregnant if the guy "pulls out in time." Second, don't try to be funny, because this will just make things more awkward. As a therapist, I find humor helpful in these talks, but as a parent I agree with Johanna. Don't be dark and stern, but, at the same time, sex is too delicate for a mom and pop stand-up routine. Just think "casual" to set the right tone. Johanna suggests never bringing up sex while riding in a car because the teen may feel trapped. I'd never thought of that before. Best of all, she suggests that instead of a graphic description of how sex works, "impart your values, but realize that we might have to learn from our own mistakes. Just give us all of the information we need to be safe." I couldn't agree more. The mechanics are well covered in many books. The values are at issue and the last place you want your teenagers learning them is on the Internet and TV.

It's never too early to begin having The Talk. The sooner you start, the more comfortable both of you will be as your child ages and you become more practiced. If it's just too hard to do it yourself, find an adult friend, youth leader, therapist, or other competent person who knows how to talk to kids. Another neat trick is to find several good books that you approve of and leave them in strategic locations around the house. Do this when your child is between nine- and eleven-years-old. They'll find them when they need them.

As Johanna points out, no matter how uncomfortable, the worst sex talk is no talk at all.

John Murray: We live in a sexually charged world and it won't help your children to pretend otherwise. Corporate sponsors make an industry out of sex. They study the brains of adolescents to unearth the secrets of their psychology. What have they found? Sex sells. A TV show could use wit and wisdom to attract viewers, but why bother when you could throw in a couple of scantily clad blondes? Take off your clothes and rake in millions. Immerse teens in a sex-crazed culture. Make them believe your products are the ticket to sexual utopia. Now you've created an industry.

Fortunately, you still have the upper hand. Teens who choose to put off sex consistently report that parental opinion is the number one reason for doing so. Talking about sex with your kid is an essential step in raising responsible and competent offspring. It will be awkward, as serious issues often are, but if you don't pass on your values to your children, they will look elsewhere.

Discussing sex will not cause your child to think about it. They already are. As Wes said, public schools impart the science involved but often fail to discuss issues of right and wrong. And when marketers have their say, nothing is right and nothing is wrong.

Don't limit yourself to a single talk. Sex should be a natural and ongoing discussion between parent and child. It's hard to cover all the bases in a single chat, and teenagers' thoughts and feelings change and evolve in response to the world around them. You'll find the talks become easier and your teen more able to discuss topics that might previously have been uncomfortable.

Then you'll be ready to move on to the next hard fact of life: Taxes.

Worth the Risk

Dear Dr. Wes and Kelly,

My fifteen-year-old daughter has had problems with irregular periods for some time. It's not bad, just inconvenient. For several months she's been bugging me to put her on birth control pills because "all her friends are on them for their periods." I think she is deceiving me about this and that she is really wanting to be sexually active. I don't want to condone that by putting her on birth control. Do you think it's worth the risk?

Dr. Wes: Actually, I think you're misunderstanding the risk here. It's not that your daughter may want to have sex. The danger is that she's having it and you may soon be a grandparent. We need to end the debate about whether teenagers should be sexually active. They shouldn't. But they are and have been for a lot longer than any of us have been alive. This leaves us to deal with the consequences. You are certainly free to try and interdict her sexual behavior, but the level of control and manipulation that requires is likely to create blowback in your family for years to come.

It's unfortunate that you and your daughter have such awkward communication about these matters, that you feel she might be deceiving you in order to protect herself from unwanted pregnancy. Now would be a great time to get that opened up and help guide her in a safer and healthier direction.

First, step back and try thinking differently about this for a moment. It's entirely possible that your daughter just wants to regulate her periods. I'll admit, however, I've heard that one many times and it's often a ruse. So what does that mean for you? In a worst-case scenario, she's trying to meet a critical need while attempting to make you feel comfortable and secure in your perception of her. You can take that as deceptive, or as a mature attempt to protect you from disappointment and her from shame. Only when you approach it from this angle do you become free to guide your daughter.

Whether you come to terms with your child being sexually active or not, the inevitable will happen.

For example, you can say to her, "I really appreciate that you're taking the initiative here on your sexual health. However, if you're going to be on birth control for any reason, I also want you to be fully aware of other issues like STDs, the emotional stakes involved in deciding to have sex, etc." In response she will groan, roll her eyes and say, "God mom, it's just for my period! Why can't you just leave this alone?" And you'll calmly say, "I know that, but once you're on birth control you become freer to consider sex someday, so lets have this conversation now. With contraception comes the full learning experience about your sexual health."

She may act upset with you, but in the end she'll think you're a really wise mom and will appreciate how seriously you take her.

Kelly Kelin: The risk. Whether you come to terms with your child being sexually active or not, the inevitable will happen. Of course no parent wants to grapple with their fifteen-year-old having sex, let alone unprotected sex. But the choices we make now will shape our futures.

You knew this day would come sooner or later, but you were probably hoping for later. As Wes notes, however, the trend among her friends and a great majority of teens is to become sexually active at a younger age. None of this will change if you do or don't put her on birth control. But, as a mother, it's part of your responsibility to prepare your child for all life's issues, including the good, the bad, and the ugly.

You say her reasons are deceptive. This shows that the problem is slightly deeper, involving trust between the two of you. This is the perfect time for you to begin a discussion. Explain why you feel it is unnecessary for her to be on contraception, but be sure to hear and understand where she is coming from. The teenage years are awkward enough and it's important to know when to play the parent versus friend role.

Once the lines of communication are open, some of the tension will disappear. If you do provide her with birth control, tell her that you aren't condoning her having sex, but if any questions arise, you will be there for her. The important thing is to educate your daughter and be there for her through it all.

Drawing the Line

Dear Dr. Wes and Marissa,

Whether we want to or not, my husband and I get your point about dealing with our kids having sex. But neither of us knows how to just sit at home and be okay with it. On one hand we don't want to know. On the other, if we don't know, we don't feel like we can do what you are suggesting in guiding our kids toward good decisions, especially the ones we disagree with. We don't want our kids out there on their own, but don't want to condone it like those parents who let their kids have their partners sleep over. So where *do* you draw the line?

Marissa Ballard[6]: The most important thing you can do is make sure you've expressed how you feel about your child having sex. You

---

[6] Marissa Ballard married in July 2010, four years after completing her tenure on Double Take. Her column bylines remain under her unmarried name, though she is listed as Marissa Ballard Hemenway for the authorship of this book.

can't just tell teens to wait until they're married because, while that is a great goal, it is not always realistic.

Make sure your child knows that if pregnancy or disease happens, they can come to you. If you have a girl, explain what it would be like if she happened to get pregnant.

The best tool I've devised for keeping sex meaningful at any age is the ninety-day rule.

What options would she have? If she chose to keep the baby, how much would you help? Would she be responsible to find daycare, or would you watch the baby while she was at school or work? Would you help financially? Sons need to understand the consequences as well. How would he pay for child support and afford college? Would you help him cover daycare expenses?

Have guidelines while your teen and his/her partner are at the house, like staying out of the bedroom or secluded areas without supervision. Restrictions like these can reduce behavior that you disapprove of under your roof. What goes on outside of your home, however, is really out of your control, but you can still ask who your teen is going to be with, and whether or not a responsible person or parent will be there.

While there's little you can do to change a teen's decision to be sexually active, educating and supporting your child, and having open conversations, can guide him or her toward responsible and well-informed decisions.

Dr. Wes: While not "everybody is doing it," at least a quarter of fifteen-year-old girls and 30% of boys have had intercourse. By age eighteen this rises to 68% for both sexes, and by age twenty, 90%. Regardless of what society may claim to value, very few of us wait until marriage to have sex.

Without that traditional principal of abstinence before marriage guiding our coupling, it becomes even more important for parents to help teens develop sexual ethics. So, parents who want to draw the line need to start with themselves first. Think twice before having extramarital affairs, because teens react very badly to them, particularly when they lead to divorce. Likewise, single parents often go through a string of relationships and then wonder why their kids are acting out.

With your child, you should draw a clear line at anything degrading or dangerous. In this, dialog is important, but trying to deter sex by over-focusing on pregnancy and disease is only likely to generate eye rolls. Instead, emphasize the core value that sex is important. It's not entertainment, recreation, or a rite of passage. It's a meaningful relationship between two people who are really into each other. So, draw the line between sex that supports a loving relationship and sex that's just fun and trendy.

Of course you needn't say, "I'm glad you and Joanne waited until you were really in love to have sex. I'm so proud of you." That's too personal and it condones something that, as a parent, you should view critically. Instead, say something more generic like, "I hope when you decide to have sex it will be within a loving relationship, and that you can be proud of that decision." Start these conversations *before* the age of twelve, teaching the ethics of human relationships and proper boundaries in preschool and then advancing the discussion as your child ages. It's never too early, and often too late.

By the way, the best tool I've devised for keeping sex meaningful at any age is the ninety-day rule: Don't have sex with anyone for ninety-days after you start dating. Yes, many teens and young adults find this ridiculously quaint and some parents find it horribly undisciplined. However, I can tell you that it works. It doesn't rule out being sexually active, but offers a sufficient delay in the process to really think things through.

And where teens and sex are concerned, thinking makes all the difference in the world.

Teen Sex Offender

Dear Dr. Wes and Samantha,

I read your column last year on teaching kids not to get into trouble with their sexual behavior[7]. Unfortunately, that's what we're facing right now. My son was sexually inappropriate with a younger cousin. The other boy's mom doesn't want to turn my son in for his sake and for her child's. But I think he needs more help than we can give him to

---

[7] This column can be found in Chapter 3 of *Dear Dr. Wes…Real Life Advice for Teens,* under the title "Age Inappropriate."

understand why he did this and to not do it again. What should we do to get him help and not make the situation worse for everyone?

Samantha Schwartz: While you may consider it lucky that your son will not be reported, the fact that he never gets truly punished for what he's done could have negative consequences. If he continues this behavior and winds up getting caught as an adult, the legal ramifications will be devastating. This is not something your son or his cousin can put out of their minds like it never happened.

However, I can see why reporting the incident to the authorities and going through the legal system could just put the victim through more trauma. Respecting the victim's mother's wishes does make sense.

As a loving parent, you want to help your son out of the mess he's made, but you cannot do it alone. Both he and the younger cousin need therapy. If you can afford it, offer to pay for the cousin's sessions. Both need to see therapists who specialize in sexual abuse counseling. Treatment will help you and your son discover the reasons for his actions. Consider counseling for yourself and the other mother involved. While the problem was centered around your children, this is a difficult time for both of you, and you deserve an outlet to discuss your feelings. Remember that his actions are not your actions, and while others may judge you for what he did, it really is not your fault.

Seek legal counsel immediately and before you seek therapy. This will be expensive, but it is absolutely necessary.

In the meantime, keep your son away from younger children. Investigate where children live in your neighborhood and closely monitor where he is going. Obviously, he should have no contact with the younger cousin. This may make your son feel disconnected from the family, but explain that there are consequences for what he did, and this is one of them.

It may be tempting to displace your anger about what happened onto everything your son does, but try not to. Don't act like nothing happened. Tell him what he did was wrong, and that it will take some time for you to completely forgive him. But also remember to tell him that you love him, and that you believe he can change.

Dr. Wes: Samantha hit many of the high points, especially regarding treatment. However, I'll add two realities to her excellent suggestions. First, your son doesn't have to wait until he's an adult to face adult-like consequences for this behavior. Quite commonly, district attorneys threaten to charge even younger teens as adults in order to pressure a plea agreement. Adjudicated teens are routinely put on the sex offenders registry, a much more devastating consequence that will last well into adulthood.

Second, we've known for many years that the "profile" of a teen sex offender has little to do with that of an adult offender, so teens are easier to treat and have better outcomes. However, society's model is no longer about treatment but severe legal sanction, and the law makes few age-distinctions in how it views sex offenders. As a parent, this means that you must balance protection of this victim and any future victims with protection of your son's legal rights and psychological health. That's not easy, but it is doable.

Samantha is correct. It's vital that your son get professional help. If you and the other mother fail to hold him accountable or don't help him understand and change his behavior, you're enabling it to continue. On the other hand, within twenty-four hours after you step into a therapist's office and share this story, your son will be reported to the authorities, and they will act decisively.

Seek legal counsel immediately and *before* you seek therapy. Since I have no idea who you are, I can't make a report and you are free to head straight out and retain an attorney before taking your son to therapy. This will be expensive, but it is absolutely necessary. An attorney won't make your son's problems go away, nor should that be your intent. However, the goal of social service and legal intervention is not to help your son, no matter what you may be told. Their goal is to protect victims from further abuse. I've spent a career on that same important goal, and I know Samantha has been involved in similar pursuits. Having a good attorney on day one and a good therapist on day two will increase the chances that your son gets the intervention Sam describes, while facing due process and hopefully, a measure of justice for everyone.

The burden is on you to supervise this young man 24/7 to make sure he does not reoffend while you're getting all this in place. If there are younger children in your home, send your son to his grandparents or somewhere that has no potential victims. This may sound extreme, but until you have the eyes of a professional on this young man, assume the worst.

Gay Daughter

Dear Dr. Wes and Kelly,

My husband and I disagree over how to respond to our teenage daughter's disclosure that she is gay. I think we should be supportive no matter what and he believes something is wrong with her and she needs help. Both of us don't like this, but I'm trying to be realistic. This is causing problems for our marriage and our relationship with our daughter.

Dr. Wes: Any valid answer involves psychological, religious, sociological and even genetic issues. It's been many years since the American Psychological and Psychiatric Associations considered homosexuality "something wrong" with a person, so from a diagnostic standpoint your husband is incorrect. Your daughter may well need help to think through and understand the implications of her sexual orientation, especially given your family's reaction. However, that doesn't make her much different from most teens who are in the process of exploring their sexual identities.

I don't want to start a fight with either the gay or straight communities, but it is *normal* to be uncertain about one's sexual identity in adolescence. We've long considered same-sex attraction as an expectable part of maturation. Only in the last twenty to forty years has it begun to take on a specific identity; that one is either straight or gay or bisexual, and that one would be certain about this by the time they are, say, sixteen. This may or may not be true depending upon the individual, and I would encourage kids and parents to hold off on making rash judgments on these matters. That's sort of the opposite of exploration. I've worked with gay adults who were quite certain of their orientation at age twelve. Others once considered themselves gay or bisexual in their late teens and then found they were not as they grew older. I believe them all.

A lot of emotion in your reaction will only generate more emotion, when in fact cooler heads are required.

You didn't share her age in your note, but the younger your daughter is, the more likely it is she's still trying to find answers. That doesn't mean that if you act now you can still "fix" this "problem." It means that you might consider giving her some room to breath rather than turning her disclosure into a major drama, which will undoubtedly push her away. In short, when it comes to sexuality, she's going to be who she is. She'll figure out who that is in her own time and hopefully with your loving support.

Over the course of her life, there will be a fair number of things on which you and your daughter disagree. Each time you're in conflict you withdraw some influence credits from the bank, so pick your battles wisely, especially on something this personal. If you oppose your child's choice of partners because they are gay or of a different race or religion, you are going to quickly spend almost all your capital on something you can't really influence. Better to focus on the quality of the dating partner. Is she good to your daughter? Does she have goals and aspirations? Does she share your values? These issues form much smaller targets and leave you with some real possibilities to influence how your daughter chooses to live her life.

Remember, a lot of emotion in your reaction to this will only generate more emotion, when in fact cooler heads are required. There is a higher incidence of self-harm and running away among gay teenagers. That's the last thing you want for your child. Find a good therapist—not to change your daughter's sexual orientation, but to help your family wrestle with these issues in as productive a way as possible.

Kelly Kelin: Raising a teen can be difficult enough, but raising one who strays from what you believe is morally right imposes many obstacles. The teenage years are an emotional roller coaster ride, a time of human development, self-discovery, and sexual exploration. Yet, it's highly unlikely your daughter's decision to be gay is just a phase. Homosexuality has been around for centuries. As Wes notes, many gay adults discovered their sexual identity at a very young age, and come to explore that sexual orientation once they are older. Others are afraid and confused about coming out, and closet their sexuality until they feel they are in a safe enough environment to do so.

You may not agree with your daughter's sexual orientation. However, she is still the same child you have grown to love and care for. The fact that she confided in you shows she is opening up and trusts you.

This is a difficult time for her and she's going to need both you and your husband to be there for emotional support along the way.

Don't create a barrier and shut your daughter out of your lives because of her decision to be openly gay. Even though you don't agree with her choice, you need to respect it. If you attempt to control her decisions, your relationship with her may deteriorate, and you may notice her growing adrift or angered by your negative reaction.

Instead, give your daughter comfort and let her know that you will love her no matter what. In the end, there are really only two options: lose a daughter who may grow to resent you or create a strong everlasting relationship with her.

Abstinence Education

Dear Dr. Wes and Kelly,

With all the criticism of the pope's recent comments about abstinence and HIV and the changes in our government, what do you think about abstinence education versus teaching kids to use condoms or other birth control? My kids will be at that age soon and I'm giving this a lot of thought.

Dr. Wes: It wasn't enough for Double Take to get into an argument over sexuality with the State Attorney General last year? Now you want us to take on the Pope? I think I'll pass. It's not because this isn't an important issue. It is, especially when different approaches to HIV prevention efforts are in a constant battle for the hearts and minds of the people. Rather, I'll pass because the entire argument creates a false dichotomy in place of a rational view of how people are behaving and how they have behaved throughout recorded history. In other words, those who want to teach people to resist sexual expression should realize that real life statistics are dramatically against them. Likewise, those who want to focus exclusively on making sex safer must realize that a mechanical understanding of prevention, without an ethical framework for decision making, leads to unsound reasoning and risky behavior.

While you might think this sounds a bit too philosophical, it really addresses the question you're asking: how am I going to communicate my values to my children as they enter adolescence? You can sit down with your kids and say, "You must abstain from sexual contact until age X" or tell them that they can only have sex after marriage and hope for the best. I know people for whom this has worked and, in some of those cases, preserving sexual expression for a committed adult relationship has added richness and meaning to their lives. Most, however, will not heed that advice.

You can also sit down and teach your kids all the ways sex can harm them—from disease to pregnancy to emotional bankruptcy and—offer them strategies for how to cope with each. That also works for some. But until you can pull together all aspects of sexuality—the physical, spiritual, emotional, and ethical—and help your kids understand how they interrelate, you're going to leave them vulnerable.

Asking your child to abstain sounds perfect, but that dream could be easily shattered when you end up caring for your crying grandchild while your teen struggles to finish high school.

I'm hoping over the next few years that those of us who believe in teaching a balanced perspective on sexuality can extend a hand of fellowship to both factions and move everyone toward the center. There, we can consider the value of conscientious sexual expression alongside the need to protect children from the normal indiscretions of youth.

You don't have to wait that long. You have kids who need that lesson now. Enjoy your opportunity.

Kelly Kelin: Throughout the ups and downs of our chaotic teenage lives, there comes a point when we slowly but surely make the transition from naïve child into hormone raging adolescent. Not only are kids adjusting to this drastic transition, but their parents are as well. Although it may be embarrassing to even fathom talking to your children about sex, curiosity is going to get to them one way or another. During this time of sexual discovery, it's important to help your kids through the process. Yet, you may find yourself torn about whether teaching abstinence or providing your child with birth control and condoms will be more efficient.

If you prefer for them to be abstinent, then tell them that. But realize that as teenagers we have a tendency to rebel against authority. So why limit them to only one option? As awkward as it may be for both of you, why not provide your children with condoms and birth control or a way to access them on their own? At the same time, be sure to educate your children on the downfalls of sex.

Ideally, asking your child to abstain sounds perfect, but that dream could be easily shattered when you end up caring for your crying grandchild while your teen struggles to finish high school. Is it worth the risk, or is it better to be safe than sorry?

Virginity Until Marriage

Dear Dr. Wes and Julia,

As a grandmother of seven with five teenagers, I was appalled at the answers to the question "How young is too young for sex?[8]" The appropriate age is when a male and a female fall in love and get married. Intimacy is a precious gift given to human beings by God and is not to be misused. We are not animals and should behave accordingly. We must use self-control and discipline ourselves to preserve our virginity until marriage. Many years ago, my mother-in-law emphatically said, "Sex ain't sacred anymore!" God intended true love to be kind, considerate and not demanding of its own way. This concept is good for young and old alike. Age isn't what makes the difference; it's our attitude and choice. The temptation of passion and lust play a big part in today's worldly concepts of sexuality. It's the same temptation that's been around since Adam and Eve, and will remain until the end of time.

Dr. Wes: I appreciate your faith and its underlying value system, and your desire to convey that to our readers. We always urge teens to take sex seriously, make ethical decisions, think before acting, and consider sexual choices as more than recreational. We made those exact points in the column with which you take such umbrage. You seem to prefer that

---

[8] This column opens Chapter 3 in *Dear Dr. Wes...Real Life Advice for Teens* under the title "Too Young?"

we choose not to wrestle with these questions, but answer them singularly, as you do.

Unfortunately your important message—that sex is an expression of love and should be carried within a sacred context—is lost in its tone. It's one thing to note that we can *choose* our sexual expression, which elevates us above other creatures. It's another to compare sexually active teens to lustful animals. Too often adults demand a standard of unquestioning obedience from young people, ignoring the more likely outcome of that approach—namely, that they will simply keep their forbidden behaviors secret.

> *Kids have quit believing in the idea of "us" in favor of a sort of "me and you" mentality for relationships.*

Those of us who spend our lives face-to-face with teens from all walks of life, faiths, and situations accept that we are not just obligated to convey good information. We must influence teens to trust our judgment and put that information to serious use. Otherwise we lose our audience quickly and, with it, any chance to make a real difference.

I'm a big fan of true love and marriage, and agree that sex is something spiritual. However, many young people are beginning to see it more like Groucho Marx, "Marriage is a wonderful institution, but who wants to live in an institution?" Kids have quit believing in the idea of "us" in favor of a sort of "me and you" mentality for relationships. Consequently, marriage is no longer a primary ethic for sexual expression, and it hasn't been for many years.

I appreciate your dissent and am glad to respond. However, this column remains dedicated to the real problems of our readers' daily lives, not the problems we wish they had.

Julia Davidson: The idea that sex and true love go hand-in-hand is one that many people still believe in, myself included. Unfortunately, that isn't going to change the behavior of millions of teenagers. The commitment with which you have shared your beliefs is admirable, but it can also be scary to young minds.

Teenagers seek boundaries, which I assume was the original reason for the reader's question, "How young is too young for sex?" These "kids-say-the-darndest-things" questions is a method of gaining leeway by learning what we can and can't get away with. Just because we ask doesn't mean we are behaving as badly as the question might imply. It rather shows our curiosity about our limits. Depending on the specificity or seriousness of the answer, kids will respond based on whether they see the limit as reasonable or fair.

Remaining committed to only one answer (wait until marriage) pushes us backwards, because we may stay tied to a given rule and regret it later, or perhaps even bypass the rule altogether. Either way, laying down the law doesn't teach us to actually consider the situation at hand, but instead encourages us to blindly follow the rule without any critical reflection. Although marriage may be the right time for a given person to have sex, it isn't the right time for everyone.

Like Wes, I respect and agree with your belief that sex should wait for true love. However, we'd be hard pressed to convince a group of religiously, culturally and ethically diverse teenagers and parents to adopt any single approach to this decision, and we'd lose credibility if we tried. We prefer to encourage teens to think through this decision carefully, and for themselves.

4 SUBSTANCE ABUSE

Trust

Dear Dr. Wes and Marissa,

I have a problem with trusting my daughter. Her best friend's mother called to inform me that my daughter is responsible for supplying the alcohol at a recent event, yet she denies even attending the event. How can I determine whether my daughter is telling the truth or if her best friend is trying to pin the blame on her?

Dr. Wes: Readers of this column know that I'm not big on trusting teenagers. It's not that I don't like them. I do. I'm not preaching that "today's generation" is running amok and taking with them our decent way of life. I just know that the whole point of adolescence is to make yourself different than your parents, whereas our goal as parents is to make our kids as much like we want them to be as possible. There's a natural tension here and the issue of trust is often the battlefield on which adolescence is fought.

I usually suggest verification instead of trust, but in this case the situation has already happened and it's hard to know whom to bless or blame. The only thing tougher than figuring out whether you can trust one young person is figuring out which one to trust in a group, since each is motivated to lie about their errors. On the other hand, I've recently seen several cases where kids get the rap for doing things I am pretty sure they didn't do, because friends dumped on them to cover themselves.

This is why having a relationship with other parents is important. I suggest you get both girls and their parents together, sit down in someone's living room and have a talk. I would do this as a bit of a surprise so that the girls don't have a chance to "get their stories straight." Someone isn't being honest here, and if neither girl will cop to supplying the booze, I'd ground them both. But you must have the cooperation of the other parents, or you won't get to the bottom of the matter.

Some will argue that this approach is too drastic and could potentially damage the relationship between the girls. However, supplying alcohol to minors is a serious offense. It could land your daughter, her friend or anyone else involved in major hot water. I know it goes on all the time, but that doesn't mean you have to tolerate it. If the other parent is up for it, I'd try this intervention.

Marissa Ballard: Underage-drinking occurs nearly every weekend in most towns, and situations like this one pop-up numerous times in high school and college. Alcohol is readily available to most teens simply by making a phone call, and parents need to start understanding that.

Someone in your daughter's group messed up somewhere along the line and somehow your daughter was involved. She may not be the culprit this time, but if the friends she's been hanging out with were drinking, chances are she too has been drinking at some point. An allegation like this can't simply come out of nowhere. What Wes suggests is a good method, but you don't always have the cooperation of the other parents. I also think that it can be handled in a more private way, involving only your family.

Asking a few questions could help you decide what you are going to do. Has your daughter ever been in a situation like this before? Have you ever caught her drinking? Does she have a habit of lying? Behavior patterns are a key element in trusting her. If she claims she was not at this party, can she prove her whereabouts?

I know this sounds like a legal interrogation, but, as Wes notes, if she continues to exhibit this sort of behavior, it could very well turn into one someday in the future.

Prescription Drug Abuse

Dr. Wes: One of the first Double Take columns we published back in November 2004 addressed prescription drug abuse among teenagers. Since then, the problem hasn't exactly gone away. In fact, I'm now finding young adults on my caseload who played around with pharmaceuticals in high school and became severely addicted by the middle of college—going up on stimulants and down on pain meds. Not a great way to keep your life under control.

The abuse of pills has a whole different dynamic than street drugs because they're easy to conceal, hard to detect, predictable in quality and dosage, and readily available from legal suppliers. In fact, most enter the world as perfectly valid prescriptions, then get re-routed shortly thereafter. One of the biggest errors parents can make is hanging on to drugs, especially pain medications or benzodiazepines, like Valium and Xanax, after they're no longer needed. Many kids begin their pharmaceutical habit (or sale and distribution business) not at school or from the supply of some nefarious dealer, but at home, in the convenience of their own bathrooms.

Regarding stimulants, it's rare that a person comes to our clinic with undiagnosed ADHD who hasn't first borrowed someone else's medication to determine whether it works. Prescribing physicians and nurse practitioners should join with parents in staying vigilant against misuse and redirection. We require parents to administer all medications to teens, and prefer that kids not spread the news if they're taking meds. For the most part, stimulants are misused as study aids, although some kids abuse them recreationally, which, given the side effects, always baffles me.

For teens, prescriptions drugs have one additional seduction—the appearance of medical legitimacy and safety. Ben does a nice job of discussing that next.

Ben Markley: Very few things are inherently bad. For instance, we have an entire department in our city devoted to fighting fire because it destroys homes and people. However, we also use fire to warm our homes, prepare food, and even set a mood. Fire isn't a bad thing, but it needs to be used properly and carefully.

The same is true of prescription drugs. Countless people work to make the most effective drugs for specific problems, and many benefit from their work. Start using those same drugs to get high or lose weight, and you're inviting in all kinds of nasty side effects.

There's this weird mindset that because it has a doctor's signature next to it, a prescription drug is somehow less dangerous than one you get in a back alley. If you're using it properly, that's true, but it stops being medicine when you start using someone else's or taking too much of your own. And this distinction isn't just limited to prescriptions. Chug a bottle of over-the-counter cough syrup, for instance and if it has dextromethorphan in it, you could start having hallucinations, along with a handful of other bad side effects.

Bottom line: Use drugs the way they're prescribed. That's kind of the point of a prescription.

Peer Pressure

Dr. Wes: I've long pooh-poohed the whole idea of peer pressure. A fair amount of research backs me up, suggesting for the most part that the role peers play in decision making is not nearly as great as that of the family. I realize that your child's pink striped hair and lip piercing might not remind you of yourself in any way, but in the long run, kids tend to revert to the influence of the home—both good and bad—rather than continuing to live out the trends of their teenage years.

There's no evidence that teaching kids to "just say no" to peer pressure does much good, or that programs on the evils of drug use or sex do more than make kids curious.

Most teens have agreed with me that decisions to drink, do drugs, steal, have sex, etc. are their decisions and nobody else's. I've even had kids argue with parents who see their friends as the problem, reminding them, "Nobody made me do that, Mom! It was my choice, Dad," while the bewildered parents wonder why the kid isn't trying to blame someone else, like they are. Kids generally understand freewill and know that peer pressure is more of an excuse than an explanation.

But now I'm starting to wonder. Teens increasingly report that their peers don't simply pressure them, but *demand* that they participate in things they aren't always thrilled about. Some girls insist that peers start having sex. It doesn't matter much which random boy might be waiting on the sidelines to meet that need, it just needs to get done. Teens report getting pestered constantly with comments like, "Oh, I'm gonna get you so high this year. Just wait!" in a tone that's equal parts fun and menacing. This kind of jocular teasing goes on day in and day out, and gets pretty annoying, from what I've heard. I've also worked with the kids who do the pestering and they see nothing wrong with it.

Here's my theory about this, which is shared by a growing cadre of teenagers. Sex and substance abuse are no longer experimental. Shoplifting is no longer a criminal act. What used to be rebellious and reckless is now common and passé. No, "not everyone is doing it," but a whole lot are, meaning that those who do not partake are in frequent, direct contact with those who do. I think the involved teens are getting increasingly uncomfortable with the uninvolved, because it forces them to consider the gray areas they'd prefer to ignore. For these kids, involvement is a matter of dogma, and anyone who isn't signing up is questioning the faith. In sociology, we refer to this as "stigmatizing deviance" in order to control it. The deviant is the non-participant in this case. So, any semblance of the groovy old "live and let live" attitude gives way to the demand that kids conform to the social norm.

I still believe the model parents set will win out by early adulthood. But there's a long road lying between here and there, which we call adolescence. There's no evidence that teaching kids to "just say no" to peer pressure does much good, or that programs on the evils of drug use or sex do more than make kids curious.

Those values need to come from the home, where parents express a clear set of ideals and behaviors surrounding these issues. And when teens cross those lines, they need to face natural and logical consequences.

Ben Markley: Does peer pressure exist? Yes. Is it dangerous? Yes, but I would argue that there is an even more powerful factor that gets less attention in most junior high health classes: peer influence. Where pressure is direct and deliberate, influence is subtler and often unintentional. It's one thing for your friends to tell you to have sex and another for them to always talk about recreational sex like they're discussing the weather. Pressure bangs at the front door and demands that we change our minds. Influence can sneak through the back and change our minds before we realize it.

Influence is more difficult to combat because it's more complicated than just saying "no." Fighting a negative influence requires a firm sense of what you really believe and why you believe it. Influence often wins out because it exposes the fact that we really don't know why we live the way we do. If your only reason for staying drug-free is because "you just shouldn't use drugs," then don't expect that reasoning to hold up when it's challenged, directly or indirectly.

My defense against peer influence is not to pull away from my peers but to reach out to my friends. Friends are one of the greatest combatants against whatever pressure may exist. That's the positive side of peer influence. Peer pressure thrives on weak resistance. Once you add enough people to the opposition, the pressure begins to crumble. If a friend pressures you, find a different one to back you up. Even if the pressure continues, it's going to have a harder time taking down a two-person resistance.

For parents, this means not just telling your kids what's right and wrong but also telling them why. An idea with a good foundation is far better than one that's been beaten into place repeatedly with the same circular reasoning. For teens, this means taking a look at our beliefs and their roots. How many of our beliefs are actually just assumptions? If we find no root, now is the time to plant, to turn to those wiser than us and ask for clarification or guidance.

Our roots are important. If we become satisfied with weak roots, then the belief they support topples over. Instead, plant strong roots, which starts with self-reflection.

Online Addiction?

Dear Dr. Wes and Marissa,

I saw an article or heard something on the radio claiming that there are actually treatment programs—like twelve-step groups—being set up for video game addiction. Is this something we as parents should really be concerned about or is it another example of the media hyping something or mental health people looking for a new market?

Dr. Wes: Initially I had the same reaction, wondering whether drug companies would now market a new medication that "reduces the risk of your teen becoming addicted to Xbox by increasing serotonin in his brain," or if schools would begin offering Gamers Anonymous as a club. After all, video games, which appeared when I was in high school in the early 1980s, have been blamed for everything from teen crime to carpel tunnel syndrome—sometimes with evidence and often without.

That said, some reasonable concern is warranted here. It seems the British are ahead of us on this issue. According to the BBC (and most teen boys I see), the new wave of 21st century games are far more sophisticated and thus a bit more intoxicating than their predecessors. Mark Griffiths, professor at Nottingham Trent University and video game addiction expert, claims that these new games are more psychologically rewarding than ever because "they require more complex skills, improved dexterity, and feature socially relevant topics and better graphics." Based on simple brain science, any increase in "psychological reward" comes with a greater risk of addiction. This is why chocolate cake is more addictive than green beans.

As with all indulgences, the problem runs the gamut from minor to severe with only a few teens reaching the point of addiction. A study of children in their early teens found that almost a third played video games daily, but only 7% played for at least thirty hours a week. It's this latter group that has clinicians and researchers worried. Professor Griffith suggests the following warning signs of video game addiction:

- Playing almost every day.
- Playing for long periods (over four hours at a time).
- Playing because one needs the excitement.
- Becoming restless and irritable if they can't play.
- Sacrificing social and sporting activities to play.
- Playing instead of doing their homework or going to work.
- Attempting to cut down their playing but can't.

This list should sound familiar. It's roughly the same criteria we use for recognizing alcoholism. From a clinical standpoint, I absolutely *have* seen teens who are addicted to video games, particularly Massive Multiplayer Games like *World of Warcraft*, which apparently is a government plot to infiltrate our brains and pacify us like something out of Huxley's *Brave New World*. If you don't get that reference, you're spending too much time playing it. This game must be more interesting than sex, romance, drugs, or music, and way better than going to school or work.

Bottom line: In considering your teenager's video game usage, keep an eye both on the emerging research and the above-cited points of reference. This addiction probably won't gobble up the world, but neither is it a joke nor the latest subject of media hype.

Marissa Ballard: I have found that those who seem to be the most "addicted" to video games are my male peers. I try earnestly to understand why sitting in front of a screen for hours every day is so wonderful, but so far, no luck. That doesn't mean I never play a game here and there, but I find myself bored and antsy after about twenty minutes. I'd rather spend time with other people.

It sounds funny to say, but I honestly believe video games can be addicting. I've witnessed several examples of it with my friends. I even know of a young man who flunked out of college because he spent every day playing *World of Warcraft* instead of going to class and studying.

For those who found the signs of addiction Wes listed to be all too familiar, it's certainly time to wean yourself off the computer or TV screen. If you're spending more than an hour or two playing every day, it's time to consider doing something else. The easiest way to do this is to find people who do not like to play video games and spend your newly found time with them. Search for a different activity that interests you. Not only will this lifestyle change benefit you physically and mentally, but socially too. It's hard to make good friends when you're only speaking with people in cyberspace.

Drinking at School Dances

Dear Dr. Wes and Marissa,

My mom and I want to know your thoughts on the recent drinking situation at an area high school dance, and how the school is handling it by requiring breathalyzers before students can enter the dance and interrogating those who they believe are involved, with a resource officer present?

Dr. Wes: I was surprised to learn that the school district was surprised to learn that kids are drinking before or during dances. While I understand the recent behavior was unusually raucous, drinking in such situations is so common it's a cliché—appearing in this column, hundreds of movies, and most popular culture. That doesn't make it okay, just commonly problematic.

The school's response needs to be deliberate and focused, not a knee-jerk reaction that will only trivialize the larger issue. For example, will the district also consider the extent to which substance abuse is a part of daily school life or other school events? Marissa actually wrote an article about this (specifically, student cocaine use) for her school newspaper last fall.

Parents must discuss with their teens how to respond to inquiries by school or law enforcement regarding illegal behavior.

In the last three years I've actually seen an increase of students complaining that substance use and distribution at school is detracting from their learning. Imagine that, teenagers complaining about the adequacy of their academic environment! So, there are certainly more issues here than the one on the table.

I think caution should be used when deciding to make dances less palatable for teens, although this could come from too little security, as Marissa notes, or too much. Believe it or not, I used to be a radio DJ and owned a mobile sound system. I did about 250 dances between 1982 and 1988 and saw all the expected problems with discipline, alcohol, drugs and a lot of really bad hairstyles. Most schools handled those problems on the spot by calling parents and ejecting kids (for the behavior, not the hair). So, these issues are not new and schools should be adept at dealing with them.

However, trying to make dances perfectly alcohol free may kill the idea entirely. Better in my view to enhance crowd control and return those who appear intoxicated to their parents, who I hope will shell out the consequences. I also worry that front end use of breathalyzers will actually increase drinking *after* students have arrived and passed the test. Thus, to be really safe teens would also need to be tested before they leave to drive elsewhere. Moreover, the school should be aware of the significant level of marijuana and prescription drugs use among its student body. It would be problematic if the breathalyzer plan actually increased the use of more easily concealed substances.

Finally, parents must discuss with their teens how to respond to inquiries by school or law enforcement regarding illegal behavior. A parent should be present if a child is being interviewed about any matter of serious disciplinary concern. Teens should consider, "If you don't tell us the truth, we're going to call your parents" an invitation they want to accept, especially if a resource officer is present. Teens and everyone else have constitutional rights, one of which is the right to remain silent and not incriminate one's self. It is an error of policy when several adults shakedown a lone teenager, especially with an officer present, without offering or demanding to call the parents. It can also be very traumatizing.

Parents should establish an understanding with their kids that no matter what the situation, they will intervene to ensure that due process is afforded. This *does not* mean a badly behaved teenager simply gets off the hook. He or she may well get into serious trouble and a parent who does not deliver or support consequences is an enabler. It does mean that the youth's rights will be protected, a rule of law that each of us should hold dear.

Bottom line: Parents need to be involved with their kids and their school, and vice versa, and should serve as the primary enforcer of substance abuse boundaries and a protector of their children's rights. As for the exact means to this end, there is plenty of controversy. As you can see, even Marissa and I don't quite agree.

Marissa Ballard: Drinking at high school dances? There's a shocker! The level of alcohol use is one of the reasons some students avoid dances all together. There have been countless instances involving intoxicated students at dances and at sporting events during my high school career. The only reason people are shocked now is because the administration is finally taking some action to stop it.

Some students argue that the schools should allow kids to be drunk at activities because it prevents them from drinking at other locations and then driving around. This viewpoint frustrates me to no end. Why cater to someone's stupidity? Follow the laws. It's not that hard.

Breathalyzers will decrease the amount of drinking before the dance. There's no way around it. Whether that will mean more people trying to sneak alcohol into the dance is arguable. This will have people up in arms as to whether it violates privacy. In my mind, it does not. It may be an inconvenience, but it is a necessary one.

I for one am thrilled that the district is finally implementing this proactive policy. While the concern that the student attendance at school functions will decrease has been mentioned in the school hallways, I doubt these grumblings will last. Eventually, people will come to accept the policy and learn to be sober at school events.

Drug Testing

Dear Dr. Wes and Samantha,

As a divorced parent of a high school student, I need your ideas on how much I should chalk up my child's behavior to simply being a teenager and when I should step in and be the parent. Specifically, how do you view the home testing of pot use? If you get a positive UA, what are reasonable consequences? What about suspending driving rights? How long is long enough?

Samantha Schwartz: If you suspect your teen is using pot, you have a right to do a home drug test. It's your house. Your teen should live by your rules. Don't just threaten to administer a test, however. If your teen knows ahead of time, she could try to tamper with the results. If the test is negative, try again a few days later. After the third random test, admit that you were wrong. If the test is positive, don't jump straight to punishment. Anger usually won't get you anywhere in helping her reverse the habit.

Instead, ask some questions. When did your teen begin smoking pot? What is the frequency of use? Which of her friends smoke? Where did she get it? Assure your teen that you will not report the dealer. You just care about her safety. If she refuses to answer your questions or shows no improvement in drug tests after three weeks, take her to a drug counselor. Hold all her money (allowance and/or paychecks) in a fund that will be waiting when she tests negative for three weeks. As a

> *It's a pretty silly state of affairs when we expect teenagers to have better judgment about drugs and alcohol than we do as adults.*

minor, your child only has rights to the money you allow. Cutting her off makes it much harder to buy drugs.

Grounding your teen won't prove helpful, because she will probably just sneak out. However, if you know she's been driving under the influence, a suspension of driving privileges is appropriate. All of these punishments should last three weeks. Experts say it takes twenty-one consecutive days to make or break a habit. Throughout, make sure your teen knows you are on her side. However, tough love is certainly needed. She is looking for direction, and you can give it. Be an active parent. Don't ask prodding questions with a suspicious air. Just ask about how her day and her plans for the weekend.

Be firm in your stance that drug abuse will not be tolerated in your house, and make sure your ex feels the same. A united front is very important. If you or your ex won't cooperate, consider renegotiating the custody agreement.

Dr. Wes: I second Samantha's advice. I have no problem with drug testing, as long as you've reached a point of reasonable suspicion, meaning you have sufficient evidence that your child has a substance abuse problem. Absent that, however, I wouldn't encourage drug testing. Unfortunately, there are about as many obstacles to Samantha's suggestions as one can imagine.

At the top of the list are adult substance abuse patterns, both in the family and in society in general. It's a pretty silly state of affairs when we expect teenagers to have better judgment about drugs and alcohol than we do as adults. I consider parental use problematic if it includes routine use of illegal drugs in the home or drinking to the point of intoxication and/or acting that behavior out in front of kids. Same with drunk driving, whether you get caught or not. If you or your ex struggle with substance abuse, you'll be fighting an uphill battle with your child. I've repeatedly seen families who spend incredible amounts of money on inpatient drug treatment for their kids and nary a dollar or a minute addressing their own chemical dependency problems. I'll let you guess how that turns out. Which brings us to the next obstacle.

Follow through. Sam is right, you shouldn't go around *threatening* drug testing or counseling or AA, or anything else. You have to stick tenaciously to these programs or else things will quickly fall apart. Some parents are at one minute bent on doing anything necessary to deal with the problem, and in the next, looking the other way. That simply won't work.

Before you do anything, make an honest assessment of the risk your child faces and your willingness to take countermeasures over the long haul. More kids are smoking weed these days than you may realize. For many it's gone from being an interesting diversion to a daily way of life. In my surprisingly controversial opinion, that isn't turning out so well.

In fairness, for many kids pot use remains recreational and its impact minor, unless you get caught. You can easily tell those kids from the "lifestyle" kids because they don't build their whole day around smoking. It's tricky to determine if you aren't hanging out with them every day, but if your kid really fits better into the first category, then you may create more problems than you solve by cracking down. But the minute a teen's pattern leans toward regular use and away from an occasional trip down marijuana lane, be ready to respond.

By the way, there are plenty of other drugs floating around, from prescription meds to cocaine. Don't hesitate to respond to those. They don't take long to exact a heavy toll.

5 MENTAL HEALTH

Stress!

Jenny Kane: A few weeks ago, Wes asked me what I thought was the single most important problem facing teenagers. I said stress. He asked what made me think that being a teenager today is any more stressful than it was for him or our parents. Of course, previous generations have had to deal with relationships, breakups, whether to go to college or not and if so, which one, to say nothing of worrying about what to wear or how to deal with family conflict.

We are raised in a culture of fear. This is our time to learn and grow, not become submerged in anxiety.

But for today's adolescents, stress doesn't come from being unable to get to your locker before class or worrying about not finishing your chores. It comes from growing up, the constant pressure to lose your childhood innocence and plan for the future. With each year, teens experience the pressure to act older than they are at a younger and younger age. Where did the sandbox, the tire swing or the tetherball go? We are shuffled about with higher and higher expectations. Just because we have better technology and information at our fingertips doesn't mean that we don't get stressed over not doing our research paper on time. It means that we will spend hours taking advantage of technology and hanging out with our friends, and, at the last minute, wind up churning out a paper that we won't even remember we wrote three weeks down the line.

Even though ours is the so-called age of acceptance, are we really that open? If so, are we better off for it? Or has it simply created a Pandora's box of stress? Is the pressure of growing up making us lose those valuable life lessons from the childhood playground far too soon? We may have everything (cars, iPods, clothes), yet all the stuff in the world can't reduce our stress. We're told to go for walks, listen to music or even scream into a pillow, yet most teens just bottle up their feelings.

It isn't our peers getting us tied into knots, it's society. It's the fact that people forget we are raised in a culture of fear. This is our time to learn and grow, not become submerged in anxiety. When we keep trying to act like adults, we—and sometimes our parents—forget that we're only teenagers, that high school is just four years of our life, and we should not be held to standards we may not be ready to handle.

Dr. Wes: Wow. Jenny is on a roll. I think I understand why she picked this topic, and the family psychology literature tends to support her. In his book *The Hurried Child*, David Elkind made the same argument, suggesting we are expecting, or imposing, too much too soon, forcing our kids to grow up too fast, as we "step-up the assault on childhood" in the media and schools, and at home.

Marilee Jones, Dean of Admissions at MIT, agrees and has become a chief opponent of the college application frenzy[9]. In fact, she travels the country lecturing parents to lighten up on their college bound teens. She thinks most of the worrying parents and kids do during this stage doesn't help much down the road. It even hurts. She tells parents, "this is a public health crisis… We're training our children to be the most anxious, stressed out, sleep deprived, judged and tested, poorly nourished generation in history." While she's speaking about the college admissions process, the same is true for many other aspects of high school. She concludes her talks by declaring, "It's not about getting into the right college, it's about becoming an adult with integrity."

---

[9] Ironically, a year after publishing a book entitled *Less Stress, More Success: A New Approach to Guiding Your Teen Through College Admissions and Beyond* (American Academy of Pediatrics, 2006), Jones resigned when it was learned she had fabricated her academic degrees on her 1979 MIT job application. In my view, this only underscores her original point.

On top of the increasingly anxious march to adulthood that Jenny, Elkind, and Jones point out, today's teens are subject to the very abundance of choices they face. Not only is there so much to do for school, but there is probably too much to do after school, some of it constructive, some of it not.

So here are a few suggestions to manage all that stress:

- Set realistic expectations based on your child's ability and unique situation, not some abstract standard or comparison to some other person.
- Kids need to get more rest and exercise. The sleep habits of the modern teen have gotten even worse than when I was sixteen, and they weren't great back then.
- The main chore of adolescence is to succeed at it. All other chores are secondary. So, a functional family is *not* determined by whether the dishes are done and the cat box is clean.
- Parents who have high expectations also need to be highly supportive. We call this authoritative parenting and it is by far the most successful kind.

A good place to start learning harmony in life is during the tumult of adolescence. School, social life, family, and the rest of the world all have to co-exist for kids to grow less stressed.

Suicidal Thoughts

Dear Dr. Wes and Julia,

How can I tell if my teen is thinking about suicide?

Julia Davidson: I'd say that everyone thinks about suicide at least once in his or her life. For some, it's a fantasy way out or a means to enact revenge. Most of these thoughts are sudden and fleeting and without consequence. It's easy to dream of a way out when stress, loneliness, hormones, or school take their toll. The people who think or fantasize about suicide and those who follow through differ greatly in number and mindset. For those watching, though, it's easy to confuse the fine line between the overly stressed, genuinely depressed person and the person who has decided that suicide is the only option.

Every teen goes through periods of feeling overwhelmed. Part of maturing is learning how much to do and how much you can get away with not doing. These times pass and by going through them, teens learn what they're capable of. However, feeling genuinely hopeless and miserable is more than just stress. It could signal depression.

If you're worried, determine whether your child's thoughts sometimes turn to suicide, and when they do, ask your child to reach out. Let them know someone cares and will listen. Know that for your child "thinking about suicide" is sometimes only thinking, and give yourselves a pat on the back for being concerned enough to ask.

Dr. Wes: The problem with any list of warning signs is that it invariably misses some individuals, while including numerous items that are symptoms for a host of other problems. With that in mind, I typically use three lists drawn from the American Academy of Pediatrics. The first includes the most serious but obvious signs:

- Any history of previous suicide attempts or strong ideations.
- Inexplicable gifting or surrendering of valued possessions.
- Talk of suicide, even in a joking way.

The next list is more ambiguous, but useful when you see several signs and the teen also exhibits a symptom from the first list, or when she has undergone some of the stressors listed below:

- Writing or drawing pictures about death[10].
- Diminished quality of schoolwork.
- Withdrawal from friends and family members.
- Running away from home.
- Appearing bored or distracted.
- Rebellious behaviors or problems with the law.
- Changes in eating habits.
- Dramatic personality shifts.
- Changes in appearance (for the worse).
- Sleep disturbances.

---

[10] This item might belong on the first list, but in today's age of anime and video games, it can create a lot of "false positives" when considered by itself.

- Difficulty getting along with others.

The final list comes from research on teens who attempted suicide. If one or more of these conditions is present in your teen's life and symptoms from the above list are emerging, raise your level of concern immediately:

- A history of violence in the family.
- Breakdown of the family unit (divorce, separation, estrangement, etc.).
- High demands to perform and achieve in school, sports, etc.
- Substance abuse.
- Loss of a family member, romantic partner, or other significant figure.
- School failure.
- Diagnosis of bipolar disorder.
- Close relatives or friends having committed suicide.
- Family alienation, including the feeling that one's family does not understand him/her or that parents have denied or ignored attempts to communicate feelings of unhappiness, frustration, or failure.
- Uncertainty about sexual orientation or having identified oneself as gay, bisexual or transgendered.

Beyond any list of symptoms, successful identification of suicidal feelings requires *communication*. This is the opposite of family alienation because it represents the necessary lifeline that helps teens share these thoughts and get help. For many families these years seem marked by distance between parent and child, but research is clear on the importance of family involvement in teen life. The key to understanding any issue, including self-harm, is not a list but a solid, rational, and meaningful conversation with your son or daughter, and making that a matter of routine beginning in early childhood.

Finally, kids often fear discussing suicidal feelings because they believe they'll be locked up, ridiculed, not believed, or left unsupported. If you believe your child is at risk, get him or her in with a therapist who is used to dealing with these issues and can further assess the situation.

Not Enough Sleep

Dear Dr. Wes and Ben,

I remember a column you did about sleep, and how much more teens need than they get. Ever since my son started junior high, he doesn't sleep well. This is more than just staying up too late; he genuinely can't get to or stay asleep. Do you have any tips to help him?

Ben Markley: I'm no expert, but I've had trouble getting to sleep plenty of times throughout my life. Here are a few things I've picked up. Follow a consistent pre-bedtime routine. It's a good way to let your body know that it's going to shut down soon. For

The worst thing about sleep problems is that they are self-perpetuating. The worse you sleep the more out of rhythm you become, then the worse you sleep.

example, I always do some reading before I go to bed, and I find I have a hard time sleeping if I skip that step. A regular bedtime, however childish that may sound, will also help.

Your son might try listening to something while he's in bed. My dad works a night shift and uses a sound machine, and I listen to audio books. He might also try soothing music.

When you've been lying in bed without sleep for a while, it may be best to get up and not go back 'til you're good and tired. This will keep your body from getting accustomed to lying awake in bed and more used to sleeping there. Sleep is an individual thing. The key to getting good sleep is finding what works best for you.

Dr. Wes: Few things impact general mental health more than sleep. Poor sleep can cause or make worse just about every psychological problem children, teens and adults face. Ben hit the high points for maintaining "good sleep hygiene" as we say in the biz, so I'll suggest another intervention before recommending the big guns.

Teenagers won't like me saying this, but a major cause for poor sleep is too much stimulation in the hour leading up to bedtime. This includes anything exciting—video games, Facebook, suspenseful movies, an emotional text exchange. Even homework can overdrive your son before he hits the sack. In fact, it's really best if the bedroom is just a bedroom, free from distractions, electronic or otherwise. When those of us over thirty-five were kids, this was taken as gospel. Now, we seem to think a properly-outfitted bedroom should look like Mission Control.

If you've covered all the issues we've already noted and your son is still struggling, it's time to determine whether he has a sleep disorder. This could range from sleep apnea to an anxiety disorder to primary insomnia, with several other possible issues in between. Sleep clinics can diagnose specific sleep problems, and that might be a good place to start. You could also take your son to a couple of sessions with a therapist experienced in working with teenage sleep problems. It won't be a deep or scary discussion. Just an evaluation to figure out what gets in the way and how to get around that. There are supplements and medications that can succeed when all else has failed.

Stick with your gut concern on this and work to correct it. The worst thing about sleep problems is that they are self-perpetuating. The worse you sleep the more out of rhythm you become, then the worse you sleep, and so on.

Psychopharmaceuticals

Dr. Wes: Recently, someone caught me on the street and asked whether psychiatrists or psychiatric nurse practitioners aren't a bit too quick to prescribe medications for kids or adults. I'm not a prescriber and I won't second-guess anyone's practice of medicine, but this comes up frequently in therapy from a more social and psychological stand-point.

When you look at the big picture, the most glaring problem with psychopharmaceuticals is not determining whether their much-needed lifelines or the marketing tricks of big corporations. Instead, what parents need to consider before putting kids on medication is much more basic: what exactly are we treating here?

There are teenagers and even children who have a genetic pre-disposition to depression, bipolar disorder, ADHD and, rarely, even psychosis. We really don't know the rates of each of these illnesses in the general population because the science is still evolving and only now are mental health services more available to the general public. Without a treatment regimen of therapy and medication, these young people will needlessly suffer. That's not an opinion; it's borne out in countless studies.

Other kids who are depressed, emotionally distraught, or behaviorally disordered are responding to problems in their environment. Sometimes medication is requested or suggested as a way to resolve symptoms which are actually behavioral displays of these problems. Some families, desperate for some level of behavioral control, seek medication.

In other cases, a teen is depressed because of significant life changes—a divorce, problems with friends, family conflict, abuse, or personal losses. While medication can be helpful for temporary symptom relief, it may actually prevent the teen from dealing with the problem and, more importantly, learning *how* to deal with problems. Instead of spending some time reflecting on whether our lives are moving in a productive direction, we often find it easier to reach for a quicker, more comfortable solution.

I recall a case many years ago where a woman was in a battering marriage and came to the session saying she'd gone off her maximum dosage of Prozac. I told her this didn't sound like a very good idea. "Yes, it is," she said. "I need to go off it because I don't think I should feel this good when my life is this terrible." She was right. Only after she let herself feel how bad things had gotten could she make the tough decision to leave an abusive marriage.

The National Institutes of Mental Health (NIMH) used to recommend that families undertake twelve sessions of psychotherapy before starting teens on antidepressants. Now, they recommend combining medication and therapy right off the bat. I still lean to the old standard in uncomplicated cases.

Either way, meds alone are not enough because symptom reduction isn't the same as problem resolution.

Julia Davidson: I'm torn on this issue. On one hand, I silently curse those people who seem to flaunt how many medicines they take and therefore how many problems they have. On the other, it seems like a poor choice not to take a medicine knowing that it will make something better. The best case is finding a middle road between knowing when to cut back on hypochondriac tendencies and when to accept the evidence that medicine is a pretty decent remedy nowadays.

I also wonder whether doctors are too quick to prescribe medicines to people of all ages, but I suspect it's because patients push so hard for them. How much and what kind of medications patients receive is largely in their control and is determined by how they describe their symptoms. Sometimes medicine can be a way of getting attention or showing bravado ("Oh, I took so many ibuprofen for my headache"). Or it can be an expression of worry that only medicine, and lots of it, can fix a problem. There's also the exaggerated diagnosis, which causes a small and easily fixable problem to escalate into a pharmaceutical nightmare. And then, of course, there are the people who like to abuse medicines for the effect it has on them. Still, others want to over-treat problems so that they feel they are getting somewhere faster. It's the elevator button effect: the more you push it, the sooner you think the elevator will come.

Just as serious are those people who avoid medicine altogether out of a fear of some complication. People aren't necessarily in control of their illnesses or problems, but they can certainly control how they handle them.

Overdosing, or refusing to dose, isn't the wisest way to handle problems. Learning about the causes and solutions is.

Cutting

Dear Dr. Wes and Jenny,

I have a young friend that cuts herself when she is upset. I would like to help her, but I do not understand why she does it. What is behind this sort of behavior? Is there anything that a friend can do to help convince her to stop doing it?

Jenny Kane: I've had friends who are cutters and I've watched them destroy themselves and their bodies, so I understand your struggle. It's hard to sit back and watch someone you care so much about do so little to help herself. A few can't even go swimming anymore because their legs are so scarred. This week I asked them to help me understand why they do it.

I learned that what draws them to cutting is the pain. Their life hurts, but for a brief second when they are cutting themselves, all they can feel is the pain of the cut. Everything else goes away. That pain helps them keep all other pain in check. The stresses, the anger, the past memories all vanish with the first drop of blood. Self-mutilation enables forgetting. It isn't for show and tell. It isn't for sympathy. It's for that one moment where nothing else matters except the blade splitting your skin. It is a release, but the wrong release. Cutting is also addictive. Everyone I talked to about this says it gives them a rush.

No matter how often she says nothing is wrong, your friend needs support and to know how much seeing her this way confuses and upsets you. She needs to realize that people are out there ready and willing to help her bear the emo-

Cutters often see themselves as emotionally disconnected from families whom they perceive as having unbearable expectations.

tional pain of life, and that there are better alternatives for coping. Encourage her to get help from someone who can listen, maybe a counselor.

I am proud of you for taking the first step in helping your friend. If you want to understand more on this topic, I recommend the book *Cut* by Patricia McCormick.

Dr. Wes: Research and clinical experience support Jenny's report. Cutting is surprisingly common, with about one in two hundred teenage girls estimated to practice it. Those stats might actually be low. While fewer boys are cutters, we've seen a rise among them too. Many adults believe self-mutilation is related to suicidal thoughts, but in reality the vast majority of cutters do not seriously consider suicide.

In my experience, and some research is bearing this out, cutting is more like anorexia, with many of the same dynamics in the home and community. Cutters often see themselves as emotionally disconnected from families whom they perceive as having unbearable expectations. They feel they cannot please their parents or live up to their sibling's achievements and may cut to indirectly cope with that sense of inadequacy. Like anorexics, cutters may also feel disconnected from peers, and seek out other disaffected kids to compensate. This is how cutting becomes a peer activity.

As for the addictive potential Jenny cited, cutting quickly releases endorphins into the bloodstream, soothing unpleasant thoughts and feelings or providing a mild high. Simply put, habitual cutters become addicted to their own brain chemistry, and the fact that more and more scars are appearing on key areas of the body, is insufficient reason to stop.

As for helping your friend, speak to her parents and encourage them to take this seriously without becoming overly upset. Hopefully, they'll remember that the first rule of parenting is to *try to remain calm,* even as they need to take decisive action. Also, as with anorexia, the best treatment involves family therapy, and it's a significant error to send a cutter solely for individual sessions. I usually split it up so we do about fifty to seventy-five percent family therapy. There are exceptions, but a focus on individual work only furthers the isolation and secrecy of the behavior. Since this problem tends to be chronic, hospitalization is rarely helpful over the long haul.

The best approach in these cases is to help kids become much more overt in their expressions of anger and frustration, and then teaching families to better resolve conflicts and manage anxiety and expectations. I know that's just what parents wanted to hear, "Teach your kid to express more anger." But that's better than the silent rage of self-mutilation.

ADHD

Dear Dr. Wes and John,

I would like to inquire about ADHD testing. While my father was in the military, I was diagnosed at the age of six with ADHD and put on medication around eleven or twelve. After my father was discharged, my medical records were lost. I am now seeking to reestablish the proper diagnosis. What are the costs involved and time commitment to be retested?

John Murray: ADHD is a neurological disorder with symptoms of hyperactivity, poor impulse control, distractibility, or forgetfulness. An ADHD diagnosis can't be made on a blood test or EEG. Instead, you and those around you will be asked about your behavior and the doctor will analyze the responses. Do you have difficulty paying attention in class? Do you often feel restless throughout the day? These are the types of questions you'll be asked to make the diagnosis. Of course, some kids don't pay attention during class because they're bored. And if you feel restless, you might just need more exercise. Because there are so many factors that could be mistaken for ADHD, a good diagnosis is crucial.

Many people wonder why ADHD is diagnosed far more now then ever before. Some say ADHD is over-diagnosed, while others claim it was always present but went unnoticed. Still, others argue that it's becoming more common because of environmental or social changes. Some children diagnosed with ADHD outgrow it by adulthood.

Treatment generally involves drugs, such as Ritalin, Adderall, etc. These stimulate the areas of the brain responsible for focus, attention, and impulse control. Most research suggests that counseling for the child and family are beneficial, and changes in exercise or diet may also help.

Ask your doctor about your options. Pay attention to your own behavior and try to outline your problems clearly. Keep an open mind and be honest. Whatever the diagnosis, know that improved treatment is allowing ADHD to become easier to live with and that ADHD doesn't have to put a serious roadblock on your path to success.

Dr. Wes: While there is ongoing experimentation with PET scan technology, standardized psychological testing is the easiest and least expensive method to improve the accuracy of diagnosis. Check with area psychologists and see which ones specialize in assessing ADHD in teens. They should provide a two-page test for you to fill out, along with several other assessments for your parents, friends, teachers, or other observers to complete. This use of multiple tests allows us to assess how you perceive yourself, and how others see you as well.

There is also a computer test that I refer to as the "World's Most Boring Video Game." If you take it, you'll know why. It's fairly good at finding people who are obviously ADHD but not so good at proving that someone doesn't have the diagnosis. Using these tests along with a trained therapist's interview improves diagnosis. From there, it's a matter of whether and which medications may work, along with a very directive therapy to help you learn to organize yourself to make good decisions and be successful.

Don't allow a psychologist to over-do the testing or tell you they have a special battery of tests that nobody else has. There are no tests beyond what I've outlined that do much to clarify diagnosis. If someone wants to administer the MMPI, an IQ test, or a neurological exam, be very cautious. These are rarely needed unless the psychologist sees something more serious going on, like frontal lobe damage or unusual memory impairment. On the other hand, I wouldn't accept a diagnosis for ADHD unless I had taken the standard tests and had them scored, not just "eye-balled" by a physician or psychologist. Your scores have to be compared to the standardization sample (a group of people who took the test and to whom you will be compared) before they can be interpreted. I've seen many psychologists use unscored tests to diagnose people.

The entire cost for an ADHD evaluation should run about $150 for the initial session, between $50 and $150 for the testing itself, and about $100 for a follow up session about diagnosis and referral. Your insurance company will usually pay for the two sessions. Very few will pay for the testing. You or your family can call your insurance carrier to find out.

Pathological Lying

Dear Dr. Wes and Samantha,

We want more information about teenage lying that borders on the pathological. In addition to being bright and talented, our seventeen-year-old daughter lies, cheats, and steals. She's exhibited secretive behavior since childhood including hiding candy in her bed. In adolescence she was diagnosed with anxiety and later ADHD, and is on medication for both now. She lies about almost everything from big things to small inconsequential ones. We've caught her cheating on schoolwork. She takes things from her friends. When confronted she initially plays dumb, then gives a completely irrelevant comment that does not explain anything. She does not respect any personal boundaries, feels free to make use of items belonging to anyone in the household, and acts as though rules do not apply to her. She is a pretty and popular girl but headed for more serious trouble.

Samantha Schwartz: Lies are part of social exchange in our culture. We lie about liking awful presents. We lie to telemarketers and say we can't talk because we have company. We lie to friends about their "adorable" haircuts to spare their feelings. However, your daughter has reached a point where her lying is frequent and hurts others. She has a serious problem and may be ruining her relationships for some time to come. If you cannot help her change this behavior while you still have legal guardianship, it may never change.

As I understand it, a pathological liar is someone who lies in spite of him/herself. I have no way of knowing whether your daughter fits this description, but I'd want her to meet with a professional for diagnosis and treatment. You should follow up with the professional to make sure she has been attending the sessions.

Dealing with this problem requires a balance of support and discipline. Tell her often that you love her and make sure she understands that you're only sending her to therapy to save her from herself and the damage she's doing. Explain how dangerous it is to lose the trust of her loved ones. You have the right to be stern and punish her when she lies or breaks the rules, but always remember to keep the majority of what you say tipped toward the positive. Since you list so many assets in your letter, I'm confident you can see the good in her,

What I'm curious about is how in the world she's gotten this far without massive retaliation from you, her friends, school, or even the cops.

Finally, I hate to downplay your other concerns, but some of those behaviors—hiding candy, cheating on schoolwork, using family members' belongings without asking—are normal for teens. Also, while I believe it's wrong to cheat on schoolwork, many of my classmates have done it. That doesn't make it right. But neither is it, by definition, pathological. And yes, I'm guilty of using my sister's and mom's belongings without asking. Extreme versions of these behaviors are a different story, but on those issues, your daughter may not be as bad off as you fear.

Dr. Wes: It's called Double Take, so Samantha and I differ a bit here. I think what you're describing *has* reached the extreme. Few young people have as hard a time as those with both ADHD and anxiety. About twenty-five percent of people with one diagnosis also have the other, and they're among the most tortured folks I treat. Those symptom sets simply don't play well together and it takes an experienced therapist and prescriber, plus early intervention, to get things to come out right.

A diagnosis is not, however, the same thing as an excuse. What I'm curious about is how in the world she's gotten this far without massive retaliation from you, her friends, school, or even the cops. As Samantha notes, you're almost out of time with her as a minor, yet she seems undaunted by consequence. So, something is really wrong here and it's up to you to correct it fast.

I'd play hardball right now. She can't afford anything less than super-tough love. I'd turn her whole world into a contingency for telling the truth and playing fair. Does she have a car? A cell phone? A room in your house? A metro pass? Does she plan to go to college on your dime? If so, now would be a great time to link all those goodies to pro-social behavior. Young people who lie, cheat, and steal are violating a core social contract with their families and community. Somehow your daughter hasn't gotten the memo, so I'd start selling off her property, ASAP. That's what eBay is for. You can stop when she stops and wait a bit to see what happens.

She will push back to be sure. Maybe move out. Get in trouble. When she does, *do not* lawyer up or bail her out. She's bought her ticket. Now, she gets to ride. This won't be easy, but if things are as bad as you say, you have to take decisive action.

I agree with Sam that you need to do all this under the treatment of a good therapist. However, I wouldn't spend a dime on individual therapy. You (both parents) have to be directly involved. Of course, lots of therapists are ready to see your daughter every week by herself. But, in your case, therapy also needs to support you in maintaining a hard disciplinary line. Once she's operating less like a sociopath, the therapist can let her come in alone and discuss whatever she wants. Until then, you have to take her down a few pegs, before someone comes along (read: the court) and does it for you.

Finding a Therapist

Dear Dr. Wes and Miranda,

What tips do you have for finding a good therapist? We haven't had much luck in the past finding a suitable match for my son, but we'd like to try again. He's fourteen, if that helps.

Miranda Davis: First, talk to your child's pediatrician or doctor and see whom he or she recommends. As medical experts, doctors probably know certain therapists on a professional level and can help narrow the field down to someone whom your son can work with.

Second, ask friends and family who have gone to therapy. A patient's review of a therapist is pretty honest, and word of mouth is one of the most common ways people find their regular family physicians, dentists, etc. Schedule a preliminary meeting with your child's new therapist before your child ever meets him/her. This way you can discuss any worries you may have beforehand, and make sure you're on the same page regarding treatment plans.

Because you mentioned past difficulties, make sure you're giving any therapist you choose enough time to show results. It's easy to jump to the conclusion that something doesn't "work" after only a short amount of time. But, for both the child and the family, therapy takes time and effort. Make sure you attend family sessions and follow the therapist's advice until you have a clear reason not to.

> *Kids need therapists who capture their attention and win their hearts. If after two or three sessions there's no connection, move on.*

It is difficult to watch someone else try and take care of your child. So, remember that therapy is a medical practice. If your child broke his arm, you would go to a surgeon because you wouldn't be able to heal it yourself. There are many talented, qualified professionals out there and, hopefully, you will be able to find one who is compatible with you and your son.

Dr. Wes: Miranda offers some pretty darn good advice on this topic. However, if you follow her suggestion about going to a preliminary session without your son, you will run into two issues. The first is cost. Insurance usually won't pay for any session that doesn't include the client, and it would be very unwise for you to sign yourself into treatment if the therapy is for your son. Still, some families find the prelim worth the expense.

The second issue is much harder to overcome. While things have improved within the last ten years, some teens are still leery about therapy. That suspicion rises tenfold if they find out you've come in ahead of them, especially if the issues involve parent-child conflict.

Thus, a preliminary session is often interpreted as a huge endplay and can get things off to a bad start.

Finally, your view of a therapist's greatness may differ substantially from your son's. So, all in all, you might lose more than you gain from a preliminary appointment.

With that caveat, here's my short list of additional tips.

- Look for someone who specializes in working with teens. This is one thing you can safely do without upsetting your son. Most therapists will provide you with a résumé on request.

- Kids need therapists who capture their attention and win their hearts. There has to be a connection because therapy must be influential. For example, if your son isn't a talkative guy, the last thing he needs is a therapist who sits in silence and waits for him to speak, and some do exactly that. A skilled therapist knows how to "feel" her way through a session with a quiet kid. If after two or three sessions there's no connection, move on.

- Be sure the therapist knows how to involve you. In difficult cases, therapists should not routinely see teens without ongoing consultation with the parents. This does not mean the therapist downloads to parents everything the kid says. It means he or she advises you on how to work better with your son, and keeps those conversations above board to avoid garnering suspicion.

- Leave with specific strategies. Some therapies can drift, and in many cases that's a great journey of discovery. But the therapist should also assist in problem-solving. Rather than functioning only as a caring ear or paid friend, the best therapists tend to be "kindly blunt" when directing you and your son through your journey.

Medication Compliance

Dear Dr. Wes and Jenny,

My fifteen-year-old son was diagnosed with bipolar disorder and ADHD. His doctor, his teachers, and I all really want him to take the prescribed medication, but he adamantly refuses. This has become a constant argument for us. I was also told that I shouldn't rile him up, but that's hard to do when he won't take the medication. He is not a bad kid, just really obstinate about this. What do I do?

Dr. Wes: Med compliance is as difficult a problem as you're going to face with a teenager because even for minors it requires informed consent[11]. We see this issue not only in cases of psychological disorders but also with chronic illnesses, such as diabetes.

For this column, I'll assume your son was: (a) diagnosed correctly; (b) prescribed a medication by someone who was sensitive to the many struggles faced by teens with these sorts of problems; and (c) has had sufficient symptoms to worry you if he goes off medication. Diagnosis and prescription is a complex process, and trial and error make it more difficult to get treatment compliance because your son will see maximum pain and minimal gain from medication. Teamwork is the key to dealing with this and your son has to be on the team. If he's not, things will get a lot more complicated in a hurry. Unfortunately, the nature of ADHD and bipolar disorder among teens often leads to oppositional behavior, and refusing medicine is a major way to act out.

These medicines are intended to have a calming effect, which doesn't exactly impress some teens, especially boys. Stimulants or mood stabilizers usually cause them to feel more focused and serious, allowing them to think before they act. This sounds like heaven to parents, but for kids

It's tough for anyone to realize that he needs meds to help him through the day, instead of being able to rely only on himself to handle his problems.

it's often seen as hell, as their normal rambunctiousness is replaced with something that seems pretty blasé by comparison. One girl told me that when she was on her ADHD medicine she didn't feel like cheering for her team any more. Not so good, given that she was a cheerleader. Without it, however, she struggled to keep her grades up and remain on the squad.

You could try introducing your son to kids or young adults who are on meds and functioning well. Around here we refer to these folks as

---

[11] Agreeing to accept a treatment with full understanding of the implications it entails.

"the masters," people who have been through horrible downs, bouts of rebellion, legal problems, hospitalization, etc. They've come to see themselves as better off with a good team-based treatment than without it. Getting to know someone like that might help your son learn something without having to personally experience all the consequences.

Jenny Kane: Your son likely thinks medication will make him feel like someone other than himself. It's tough for anyone to realize that he needs meds to help him through the day, instead of being able to rely only on himself to handle his problems.

Help your son realize that his doctor only has his best interests in mind. The doctor isn't just there to numb him out, but to allow him to feel more in control. Drugs are meant to help, not harm. Sit down with your son and, in a mature manner, discuss why he needs medication, and ask why he's so resistant. If you understand his hesitation and fear, it will be easier for you to help him. Just remember to stay calm, even if he gets emotional. When you talk to him, maintain a mature disposition and treat him like an adult.

Helping a Young Adult

Dear Dr. Wes and Julia,

My daughter has always been a good student, popular, and well adjusted. Now that she's past eighteen she's beginning to have mental health issues. She is severely depressed, cutting, and tried to commit suicide a few days ago. How do we as parents help her? According to the legal system, she is an adult now, so we have no control over treatment or anything. I am grasping at straws here and need to know how to help her and show my support.

Julia Davidson: Your immediate involvement is necessary. Don't make suggestions or try and let her do it herself. Get her help. Once she is in a more stable mindset, figure out what is causing these extreme anxieties. The fact that her depression and so-called "adulthood" began at around the same time doesn't seem like just a coincidence. I wouldn't suggest saying, "you're too immature to be on your own, move back in," but try to figure out what is causing her extreme behavior and help compensate. Maybe she's taking on too many things at once, having relationship or friendship troubles, or dealing with something difficult alone. Offer to help her get things back under control. She could be nervous about supporting herself and taking on the endless responsibilities of adulthood. She may be living on her own, but she still requires help dealing with her problems.

If you just listen to her share her experiences as opposed to directly asking what is wrong, you might get a better perspective. In the end, she may just be very stressed, or she may have more serious diagnosable problems. Either way, she still needs your help as parents. The legal system may call your daughter an adult, but being eighteen doesn't automatically take someone out of their parents' care.

Dr. Wes: These cases are not uncommon and are in fact becoming more prevalent. However, they are particularly difficult, given your daughter's age and the severity of her issues. Julia is correct. Arbitrarily setting the age of majority at eighteen ignores the fact that kids aren't even out of adolescence until age twenty, and not at full brain development until about twenty-three or four. For most young people that poses little more than a rough patch on the road of life, and I'm not suggesting we need to change the law. However, adolescence and young adulthood are precarious years in which troubled individuals have most rights of the majority, but none of the maturity.

The law sets a high standard for what we refer to as an "outpatient order of commitment." The threshold is even higher for an inpatient commitment. The principal criterion for overriding anyone's rights is the danger he or she poses to self or others. The problem is proving that danger to a hospital screener—whose job it is to filter out all but the most severe and risky cases—or to a judge who has to balance an individual's rights and safety. Based on what you've said, your daughter may well be posing this level of risk to herself. If you haven't done so already, be prepared to push the issue hard at the next incident.

Though we're seeing even earlier onsets now, this is still the age when serious psychological symptoms tend to appear. Those you describe could fit with either bipolar or severe unipolar depression, or an emerging personality disorder. Only a mental health provider could really figure out which, and because of your daughter's inner turmoil, even that will take time and multiple contacts.

If you can't get a court order, the only real shot is working to maximize your influence over your daughter through other means. Many families bring their young person into treatment with the understanding that the parents will pay the bill, help keep her afloat, let her live at home and so on, as long as she participates. If she refuses, things will get dicey, but if you hold firm and she doesn't find an alternative income source or living space (use your imagination), negotiating a strict behavioral contract often works. Sometimes a lot of pressure is necessary and in other cases a gentle approach is best.

Of course, substance abuse and addiction complicate matters tremendously. Typically, distressed young people want help, whether they will come right out and say it or not. I've seen many cases that seemed terrible at first but then turned out okay in the end.

Hang in there.

6 SCHOOL

Homework vs. Study Time

Dear Dr. Wes and Miranda,

How do you get high school kids to do homework? Our son is a ninth grader and this is the first time we've had problems with getting his schoolwork done. What do you suggest?

Miranda Davis: Having an involved parent is key to success in high school. It's great that you're promoting good study habits now before your son heads off to college, because you won't be there to help him.

It's not rocket science that students don't want to do homework, but completing assignments is crucial to understanding the material and getting good grades. Sitting with your son after school and going over assignments and

Asking a young man if he has homework is like asking if he's having sex with that girl you hate.

what's due in the coming week is a great way to get him started. But make sure it's him—not you—who is keeping track of assignments. It's a small jump from parental involvement to helicopter parenting.

Also, stay in communication with teachers, but not excessively. Communicating by email and attending events like open houses and parent-teacher conferences can let teachers know that you are there for support if they ever have a problem with your child. Technology can also help. Most districts have a nifty program like PowerSchool or Skyward. All you have to do is get your account information and you can access your child's grades to check on missing assignments.

By taking these steps you are enforcing good practices that will hopefully last for the rest of your child's education. This is one of those parenting moments where your kid may not be happy with you, but in the long run he'll be thankful. Playing the "bad cop" will send the message that homework isn't optional, which will benefit your child down the road.

Dr. Wes: Asking a young man if he has homework is like asking if he's having sex with that girl you hate. He's likely to give you anything but a truthful, straightforward answer. So, I always suggest that as early as elementary school the idea of "homework" be dropped, and "study time" put in its place. Study time is a defined period of the afternoon or evening in which the student works on learning something. As classes get harder, study time increases by about ten minutes per grade level, so your son would get about ninety minutes in ninth grade. I realize that sounds painful, but as Miranda says, it's not supposed to be fun, just necessary.

If your son has homework, then he can complete it during study time. If he doesn't, you will provide him with enrichment activities via software or texts you can purchase online. One of my favorites is the list of vocabulary words for the SAT or the study guide for the ACT. If you do this correctly, your son will never again claim to have no homework because he'll have to use the time one way or another, and who wants to do homework *and* enrichment exercises?

If the student does the full ninety minutes Monday through Thursday without fail, then give him Friday and Saturday off. If you can get away with it and still get the job done, you can also give him Sunday off. If he gives you problems with compliance, just shut down the entertainment devices until study time is over, or forever—whichever comes first. There are software packages that give you controlled access to the Internet on your computers. They'll even shut down the system until you enter your magic unlocking code. Use them.

What should you do if your kid finishes early? I favor using the entire time at least four days a week. There's invariably a chapter to be read or a test to be studied for, and if there isn't, you'll provide some excellent learning opportunities so that he spends his time wisely.

College is expensive and the economy is weak. If you're going to spend the money on sending your son for higher education, hedge your bet now by giving him the tools to succeed. There's plenty of time for Xbox, soccer practice, and that girlfriend you hate. Ninety minutes a day isn't much of an initial investment for what you and your son stand to gain.

My Child is a Bully

Dear Dr. Wes and Samantha,

You've talked about how to handle bullying before. What do I do if my child is the bully? My child hasn't been exposed to this kind of treatment, so please don't warn me about that. My child just seems to like power and that isn't making life easy.

Dr. Wes: Bullying is just about my least favorite topic, but it's refreshing to get a letter from a parent concerned that her child is mistreating others. The only way this ever gets solved is to start with you. While the underlying issues aren't so straightforward, your response has to be. Samantha offers some great interactive suggestions below, so I'm going to focus on the tough love part.

Get very specific. Compile a list of complaints others—teachers, friends, etc.—have about your child's conduct. Words, actions, texts, hateful looks. Sit down and go over them item by item and state clearly that the behaviors will not be tolerated. Then lay out exactly how the consequences will go down. I find the best way to discipline oppositional kids (which bullies usually are) is to make the punishments really annoying. For instance, take away only the favored video games or DVDs and leave the ones he's bored with. Turn off text messaging, but leave the phone on. Put a timer program on the computer so it shuts itself down after a pre-set number of minutes, then meter out the time based on behavior. You can be especially hard on violent video games, not because there's any evidence that they contribute to bullying, but because you're making a huge metaphorical point by saying, "I guess you're not mature enough to understand that this isn't how real people act in society. Get back to me when you are."

Take your child out of circulation so you can spend a lot of quality time together. This solves two problems: he's not exposed to other kids and you get to reprogram him. Watch some nice movies about good and evil. Superheroes, teen comedies, Schindler's List. It doesn't matter, as long as you get to sit down and say, "Look there, your treatment of others reminds me of that prison guard. How do think his victims feel?" I realize this sounds over-the-top, but the core element of bullying is sociopathy—a lack of empathy for others, and the pain one is causing them. Media is a great resource for stepping back and seeing how these things look and turn out in a shorter-than-life format.

If she's acting out this way, now is the time to stomp it out. If you don't, I can assure you that society eventually will.

Release your child back to the community only after she can state a clear understanding of the nature, quality and wrongfulness of her behavior. Not just lip service. Be patient and keep at it 'til she does. Then keep a close eye on the situation. Make sure teachers and administrators know you're dead serious about this and that you want to know if the behavior is continuing. If your child blows it, start all over again and make it worse this time.

Bullying is almost by definition secretive, so feel free to use espionage to monitor what's going on. In other columns, I refer to this as having "reasonable suspicion" that authorizes you to step up your supervision. Let your child know that you now have the right to access his private affairs—Facebook, email, texting—until he shows himself capable of being humane to others.

Yes, it's that serious, not just for the victims but for your kid. If she's acting out this way, now is the time to stomp it out. If you don't, I can assure you that society eventually will. So thanks for taking your job as a parent seriously. The rest of us appreciate it.

Samantha Schwartz: Wes is right. What you do as a parent right now is crucial. Teach your child how to be a good friend, and discuss with her how a healthy friendship works. However, if you try to shove morals down her throat, you probably won't get anywhere. Work through this problem in stages.

Stage 1: Discuss. I know that you think your child has never been bullied, but he could have some unresolved insecurities that are causing him to behave this way. Have him make a verbal list of his favorite and least favorite personal qualities. Pay close attention to the least favorite qualities.

Stage 2: Observe. Encourage your child to invite friends over to your house, and try to stick around as much as possible. Keep track of specific examples of meanness. Also note the reactions of the other kids. That way, when she treats her friends badly, you'll have the specific examples Wes suggests to back it up.

Stage 3: Confront. Tell your child you've noticed that he treats his friends cruelly and you're worried that he will lose them. Sprinkle in examples as necessary, but don't throw them all out at once. Your child will immediately take the defensive. Ask him why he feels the need to dominate his friends and be in the power position. Is it about being popular? Is your child scared that his friends would ditch him without force? Find out who your child feels he might have hurt with his words, and discuss these regrets with him. The more he can identify right and wrong on his own, the better.

Stage 4: Plan. Help your child create a plan for change. Give her suggestions of how to make amends with people she's hurt. Talk about thinking before she speaks and offer strategies to hold back snappy, cruel comments.

If the behavior continues, consider taking your child to a counselor who can help him work out these issues and teach you more strategies for enforcing better behavior.

Not Interested in School

Dear Dr. Wes and John,

My fifteen-year-old son has been struggling with homework since eighth-grade. We have tried everything from strict to lenient schedules, tutors to counseling, yet nothing seems to get him interested in making the grade. We tried to explain the importance of good grades for college, but he just doesn't seem interested. Ever since a sixth-grade instructor told him grades weren't important, he has been apathetic about them. He told me last evening that there is a definite disconnect and he doesn't know how to get past it. He is also concerned about not knowing what his interests are, since a lot of his classmates seem to have direction and he doesn't. I suggested that he put thoughts of going to college or into the military aside for now, get a job and work for a while until he gets to a point where he has some direction. Or maybe he should get his GED and go from there. I really feel he needs to work it out differently than the mainstream. Am I on the right track and are there any other ways to help him through this difficult time?

Dr. Wes: While we can't say with certainty what may be causing your son's problem, we can suggest ways to find out, and offer a few generic suggestions to help him cope. You should start by getting your son tested for ADHD. The issues you are describing, lack of interest in school, low initiative, sense of "disconnect," lack of direction or specific interests, etc., are included in a fairly classic pattern for young people with this disorder. Unfortunately, many people still believe ADHD is some kind of plot by psychologists or drug companies to tranquilize rowdy teens. Others think it's a behavior problem and kids just need to straighten up. Research proves again and again that neither view is correct.

ADHD typically goes well beyond failure to pay attention, affecting nearly every aspect of development from school and job performance to social and family life. Sadly, many of these kids have been told useless and sometimes bizarre or hurtful things by school staff. This includes telling the child that he or she "would just do fine if he would apply himself" or saying that the child "is just 'lazy' or 'a slow learner.'" The implication is that the child has some sort of character flaw, rather than a serious learning disability that if addressed might actually allow him to reach higher and learn more. I've seen many a young person begin treatment and go from Ds and Fs to As and Bs. It's one of the great joys of this profession. So, take your son to someone who *specializes* in teenagers with ADHD and related problems and see if the diagnosis applies. There are still a lot of mental health providers who don't really "get" ADHD, so you need to see someone who can really talk the talk and walk the walk. And if this isn't the issue, a good provider will help you figure out what is.

Your forethought about college is well-founded. Many young people simply are not ready for traditional higher education at eighteen, and if your son does have ADHD, he may need a few years to settle down and get his brain past its final developmental phase. For many of these young people military service has actually been a godsend, offering structure and purpose like nothing else. So I wouldn't rule that out. If he's really interested, it could be just the ticket. While our current military situation gives me pause in offering such advice, I still find the service to be a viable alternative for kids like your son.

I really applaud your attempts to help your son keep functioning.

John Murray: Given that you've tried many options and that the problem has been progressing for quite awhile now, I doubt you will find a simple cause or solution. So, keep doing what you have been doing, patiently and systematically working through all your options.

Have you asked his teachers for their thoughts? It's likely your son behaves differently at school than at home. They might be able to notice what interests him or turns him off about school. Make sure he's involved in these talks. With his instructors there, he might find it easier to discuss his academic performance. I'll never forget my seventh-grade biology teacher who noticed I was scoring poorly. He realized the class was too easy for me and was killing my desire to work at it, so he offered me private lessons in ninth-grade biology under the condition that I make up the work I missed out on. I felt instantly reconnected with my class and my grades started to improve.

Perhaps your teachers have some "kinetic learning" ideas of their own. Unlike many European countries, America lacks a high school equivalent of vo-tech and insists on modeling all its classrooms to an "academia" style of teaching and learning. But you might be surprised at the educational opportunities available outside the classroom.

At the very least, make sure your son has a job this summer. Earning money has a funny way of instilling responsibility in people, who suddenly see the direct fruits of their labor. It may also give your son time to settle down and think about his long-term options, realizing that he is the one who must live with the consequences.

The Elusive IEP

Dear Dr. Wes and Julia,

You often suggest getting an Individual Education Plan (IEP) at school for kids with behavioral or psychological problems. We've been trying to do this for over a year and it has been awful. The school keeps putting up roadblocks. We aren't even asking for a lot of services or adjustments. We just want something in writing for our child who has some serious emotional problems. Any suggestions?

Dr. Wes: There's a lot to learn about this issue and you pretty much have to be a lawyer, psychologist, politician, school counselor, teacher, and student—all at the same time—to appreciate everything that's involved. Even a basic overview would take two hundred times the space available in this column.

Years from now you don't want to be sitting around with your twenty-one-year-old wishing you had pushed harder for an IEP.

I agree that IEPs are getting harder to obtain. Schools really are becoming more resistant to identifying kids, much less serving them. I'm sure I'll get hate mail for saying this, but I've worked numerous IEP cases over the last few years in which families had to strenuously advocate to get services from their home school, and sometimes even those efforts are not enough.

I understand why. Schools are stuck with stagnant budgets, increased societal demands, fewer involved parents, and declining real-world salaries. Nevertheless, the law (known as IDEA) is what it is and must be followed, even if that is difficult. It exists to ensure that kids who have special needs or problems—cognitive, emotional, psychological, or behavioral—aren't denied an education. Period.

I'd recommend the book *From Emotion to Advocacy* by Pam and Pete Wright. Everyone I've lent it to has come back and written me a check asking to keep it. If you've been trying to obtain an IEP for a year without results, then I'm assuming you've exhausted most of the obvious solutions. This book will offer you some alternative strategies.

If you can afford it, you may wish to consult an attorney. I'm not a fan of getting lawyered up for no good reason. In fact, those TV commercials begging me to sue someone kind of make me sick. But an education isn't something you get a second shot at. Years from now you don't want to be sitting around with your twenty-one-year-old child wishing you had pushed harder for an IEP. If you're correct in your assessment and your child needs these services to succeed, it's a good investment of time, money, and effort.

Julia Davidson: My best advice would be to have a backup plan that doesn't require all of the appointments and paperwork-based decisions that can get you nowhere. As Wes said, budget cuts are really inhibiting the number and accuracy of IEP assessments, so even if you do get one, there's no way of telling whether or not it will be followed. Here are a few ideas that may help crack the IEP problem.

When I looked up the components of an IEP, I saw that it required an "IEP team" composed of "the student's parent(s) or guardian(s), a special education teacher, at least one regular education teacher, a representative of the school or district who is knowledgeable about the availability of school resources, and an individual who can interpret the instructional implications of the child's evaluation results (such as the school psychologist)." Seeking a special education teacher from a different school or a specialist in that field might pave the way for a better evaluation and, in turn, a better program for your child. Along those lines, choosing, rather than being assigned a psychologist, a regular teacher, and school district representative might improve things.

You could also seek out and involve therapists or psychologists from outside the school to help specialize the child's program. Bringing together the people who know your child best with folks who know how to bring an IEP into action could work to your advantage. Also, depending on the extent of your child's needs, you could research programs at other schools and see whether he or she could gain anything from attending enrichment programs, in addition to regular education. Finally, if you find no help in public or private school programs, home or virtual schooling—with the help of special education teachers—might be an option.

No Pass, No Play

Dear Dr. Wes and Julia,

My son is fourteen and in eighth-grade. He has ADHD and bipolar disorder. In seventh-grade, all he'd do was sit in his room and play video games. He had only one friend. Then along came weight training and a growth spurt that gave him a boost in self-confidence. Then the track coach recruited him and he earned a spot on an invitational meet and won a medal. Thanks to that coach he came out of his room and started to enjoy life. He has now joined football, wrestling, and basketball. He's even talked about going to college. Then we heard that once he's in high school next year, the State High School Activities Association won't let him play sports if his grades are poor, which, given his problems, they will be. We were advised to put sports participation in his IEP, but the school says that won't make any difference. I don't understand how this is helpful or fair to my son.

Dr. Wes: This policy, usually referred to as "no pass, no play," is based on the notion that athletic participation can be an effective reward for passing grades. It traces back to Texas in the early 1980s, when sports so dominated some schools that kids were allowed to pass simply because they were good athletes, setting aside the real point of school. However, as even a quick check of the Internet will reveal, the policy has many critics who share your concern.

For many kids exercise for its own sake is an unlikely proposition, so the competition and team-work of junior and senior high sports is an ideal way to get the job done.

Unfortunately, as with most adaptations of psychology by politicians, this policy misses some important points, especially for kids with special needs and those on IEPs. First, we must consider whether participating in sports or any school activity actually motivates students, and, if so, how we would use that power strategically. I know of no research that actually supports this hypothesis. I can see how coaches could motivate players by benching them during weeks where their grades were poor, but that isn't the same thing as being excluded for the season.

Second, one would have to determine a reasonable level of achievement. According to the State Association you cite, all students involved in governed activities must pass five or more classes in the previous semester and be enrolled and passing five new courses not previously passed. While individual schools can set a higher standard if they wish, this one certainly isn't very high. In fact, it only pertains to the very lowest scoring students and, sadly, the ones most prone to give up and drop out. So, we'd also need to ask whether participation could save a teenager from dropping out and, if so, whether that is a worthy struggle for an otherwise failing student. Here, the research suggests that participation *does* decrease dropout rates.

The final issue is whether a child on an IEP should have this requirement waived. Your State Association does not make any exceptions or accommodations for IEP students. However, if the school recognizes a learning disability, which they have apparently done with your son, then I believe that is a significant shortcoming in the Association's policy. In fact, many states do waive eligibility requirements for IEP students.

Of particular interest is a case in Iowa in 2003 (in re: Chase S.) that reversed the Iowa High School Athletics Association's denial of eligibility precisely because athletic participation had been written into the youth's IEP. While your State Association holds that it is a privilege to participate in sports, public schools offer this privilege and should therefore accommodate your son's education. Of course, you could ask the school to modify his IEP to inflate his grades or bring the workload down to a more manageable level, but I'm concerned about the message that would be sending to him, and whether such a change would be ultimately good for his education. Instead, I suggest that you petition the state on your child's behalf for a change of policy. If enough parents do this, it could make a difference.

Finally, exercise is crucial in improving teen mental health. Our increasingly sedentary teen culture creates both physical and emotional health problems. For many kids exercise for its own sake is an unlikely proposition, so the competition and teamwork of junior and senior high sports is an ideal way to get the job done.

Julia Davidson: I agree that a piece of paper shouldn't hold your son back from something he enjoys and benefits from. However, paperwork can be a major factor in determining eligibility for a number of activities. If all the head-honchos see is a few bad grades, they will probably axe him without a second thought.

There are a few things that might help in ensuring his continued involvement in sports. First, don't take what your school says as the end-all-be-all of your son's situation. Investigate, take matters into your own hands, and only decide that something "won't make a difference" when you yourself know it won't. Wes found a lot out about this issue just by scanning the Internet. You could do the same. Read the case he cited, see if you can find any others that match yours, and see how those turned out. Using other similar stories could bolster your case.

The next thing to do is get in direct contact with the people in charge via email, phone, or letter, so you get the information directly from them. When it comes to presenting the positive effects sports have on your son, make your case so that his participation in athletics and his personal achievement *are* linked, just as you did here. Make it clear that he enjoys sports, and that he does better in social and school situations because of his involvement. Prove that sports could lead to better grades and not the other way around.

Girls vs. Boys

Dear Dr. Wes and Julia,

My son reports that when he was in school last year he felt that the teachers treated the boys and girls differently, giving stricter discipline to the boys than the girls. He felt the girls got away with more than the boys. What's your opinion on this?

Dr. Wes: In the weeks since I received this question, I've asked the boys and girls I see what they think of this scenario. Not a very scientific study, I'll admit, yet the answers were strikingly similar. Most agree that boys are subject to stricter discipline and receive more frequent punishment, but nearly all attributed this to the fact that boys act out more than girls do, instead of simply receiving differential or unfair treatment. When I pressed them a bit, several noted that girls may not be any better behaved than boys in terms of fighting, bullying, cheating, etc., but they are better at choosing when and how to challenge classroom rules. In other words, the boys make themselves targets for disciplinary action while girls are more discreet.

The real body of research and commentary on this topic is far more complicated, which is why I didn't cite it. Some argue that boys are unfairly singled out, while others believe that discipline has actually become more "feminized" in the schools, meaning less harsh and more conciliatory for everyone. Other research even suggests that girls get the short end of the stick in class by being called on less often for contributions. In short, there are probably more questions than answers on this topic right now.

A big part of the problem is inherent to the school environment. Few disciplinary procedures are effective for every kid, and in fact most work only for pockets of students. For example, anxious people have to be handled differently than bold people. Likewise, one of the weirdest things I've ever seen schools do is kick out kids who are truant. This threat only works for the few kids who really want to go to school but occasionally skip. The rest are effectively rewarded for ditching school by being freed of the obligation to go. Rarely does one disciplinary size or style fit all.

This need for more strategic intervention also applies to disciplining boys versus girls. What works for most kids of one gender may not work for the other. Yet the minute you deviate from the standard package, kids like your son pick up on the difference and seek justice, either by dialog or exploitation.

I'd try and refocus your son on what he can do to avoid getting crossed up with the disciplinary structure; or how he can reasonably advocate for himself when he can't. If all else fails, help him put things into context by pointing out that it's better to serve your time now and come out of it a better person rather than carry an "unfairness chip" around on your shoulder.

Julia Davidson: I've heard it plenty of times on TV and around my school: "That teacher doesn't like me just because I'm a girl," but rarely do I actually see that prejudice practiced. I think both males and females have made it clear that they won't stand for being treated differently just because of their gender. So, to answer your question no, I don't think boys get harsher treatment than girls.

I do think, however, that treatment and punishment alike have adapted to the times and there still exist discrimination and double standards in schools. Whether or not school administrators realize it, favoritism can become a response to discrimination, allowing people who may not have been treated as well in the past to be treated better. I've experienced both sides of this. On the one hand, being a good student might earn a little leniency on a late assignment. On the other, a student who is on good terms with a certain teacher might get treated better than me. Having been the favorite as well as the less favored student, I find neither role to be fair. The Catch-22 is that everyone deserves equal rights and treatment in the school system, but everyone also deserves individualized attention and reward for solid classroom performance. And if all it takes to earn a teacher's admiration is being nice to his or her face, then manipulation gets thrown into the game, making things less fair to everyone.

Kids should get individualized treatment and recognition based on who they are as students and people, but always in moderation and not at the expense of other students. Educators should always be aware of what behaviors and achievements they are rewarding and whether such actions truly deserve praise.

7 FRIENDSHIP

High School Divide

Dear Dr. Wes and Kelly,

Our daughter is preparing to leave her peers behind in moving on to high school because we live in a different attendance zone than all her friends. She has since rejected us and, just yesterday, told us that she hates us and isn't grateful for anything. Of course, we don't feel good at all when we hear such things, but we also know enough about how teenagers work to not take it personally. Could she be processing her feelings about her peers and what's going on?

Kelly Kelin: Your daughter is about to begin an important step in her life. The transition from junior high to high school can be difficult, especially when your friends are attending a different high school. Add in an underclassman status and not having any clue about what you're getting yourself into, and she's probably anxious and intimidated. Despite all the yelling and fighting, it's clear you're only trying to do what is best for your daughter. She may be directing her frustration at you, but it's highly likely that by the

We should help our kids adapt to new situations and challenges. However, the transition your daughter faces is not so easily made.

time she's spent a whole semester at her new high school, she will have changed her mind.

High school is a time for teenagers to really find themselves, and develop as individuals. Keep her busy with after school activities that she enjoys. This will present opportunities for her to meet new people and find her niche within high school life. You could even take some sort of recreational class together to create a stronger bond between you two and to let her know you're there for her.

Further, support her relationships with her old friends. Just because she is going to a different school doesn't mean she can't still spend time with them. Encourage her to hang out with them, set up fun things for them to do, and help her maintain a healthy balance between her past and present.

Your daughter isn't going to stay mad at you forever. When a child says, "I hate you," it is typically because they are being selfish and wanting their way. Be patient and continue to be there for her.

Dr. Wes: Kelly offers some wise words. We *should* help our kids adapt to new situations and challenges. However, after many years of practice, I've found that the transition your daughter faces is not so easily made. In many communities the high schools are fed by a set of middle schools, each of which is fed by a larger set of elementary schools. Thus, everyone matriculates together. Many districts are fairly lax about relocations so a child who moves to another attendance zone can still stay with the original peer group.

This is as it should be, in the best interests of kids, because preteens tend to enter seventh-grade with an established circle of grade school friends. Severing those relationships by attending a different middle school multiplies the core struggle of the early teen years. Usually those relationships will ebb and flow during seventh- and eighth-grade, and most teens will leave middle school with a modified or perhaps completely different social circle than the one they had when they went in. But without that initial supportive base, it's harder to enlarge and change one's support system.

By the time young people reach freshman year, they've solidified that core circle. Once again, severance brings on challenges that, at best, compete with the other tasks of high school. At worst, I still meet adults in their twenties and thirties who recount horror stories of attending a new school at one of these two transition points. It may seem melo-dramatic, but many feel they've never recovered.

Obviously, many kids make the move and come out fine, just as Kelly suggests. However, as adults, it's easy for us to think that our schools are open and welcoming places where kids can seek out new relationships and invite others to join existing peer groups. We can also imagine that by tenth-grade young people have evolved sufficient social skills and enough wisdom to face new and challenging situations. But I rarely see this rosy scenario come to pass. More and more, I've seen this forced immersion into a new social group turn out badly. That's what college is for. Pushing kids to restart their entire social network any time before that is a gamble.

Request a transfer from your current attendance zone to the one where your daughter's friends are attending. I encourage any school district to be empathic and accepting about such requests. I've seen that work out beautifully on many occasions and I bet it would for your daughter as well.

Introverted

Dear Dr. Wes and Ben,

My daughter has always been shy and now that she is in junior high she seems to prefer to do things by herself. She doesn't join extra-curricular activities or ask other girls over. When I ask if she feels lonely or wants us to help her find some more social activities, she gets mad at me and tells me that everything is okay. We need some advice on how to help her.

Ben Markley: An old Zulu adage says, "A person is a person through other persons." The English poet John Donne restated this when he said, "No man is an island." From Ubuntu philosophy to English verse, we generally agree that everybody needs somebody to some degree.

We are complementary. You have gifts, experiences, and perspectives that I do not, and vice versa. With you, I grow; without you, I put life in a box. We all know that when hardships come the heaviest burdens are the ones we bear alone. If I have no one to encourage me, to support me, to guide me, then all I can hope to do is stagger through alone until the end of my trial. We need each other.

In light of this, it's natural to be concerned for children who isolate themselves. What we must remember, however, is that no person is a project. There is a danger, especially in parenting, to manufacture a person's life based on what you think is best for them.

Children generally draw their initial worldview from their parents. A lot of kids are liberal or conservative because their parents are. Others are liberal because their parents are conservative. Either way, they are still being influenced by the parent. Kids don't want to feel as though they're being designed to think a certain way in order to complete their worth as a person. So, don't make your daughter's social life your project. Nothing will drive her into deeper introversion more quickly. Ironically, your very attempt to help her with a burden becomes a burden. Imagine if your parents had to help you with this.

Rather than approach this as a concern, try to learn from it. What has she decided to do other than extra-curricular activities? What are her interests? See what you can do to encourage and help her pursue those passions, not for the sake of her social life, but because she enjoys them. Rather than suggest an activity because it would be good for her to get out, suggest it on the basis of her interest. After all, we rarely make friends because we're looking for them. It's usually something more along the lines of, "You do? No way! Me too."

Dr. Wes: Though his advice is quite lovely, I don't completely agree with Ben and the Zulus on this one. My dad was an amateur psychologist long before I was a professional one. He taught me to hate that Barbara Streisand song, *"People...People who need people...Are the luckiest people in the world."* He felt people were entitled to be introverted if they wanted, and not get harassed by pop singers. I'm not sure that's what Babs meant exactly, but as it turns out, my dad was right—mostly. So, let's begin by defining terms.

Shy is not the same as introverted. Introversion and extroversion are on two ends of the same spectrum, not discrete ways of being, and introversion is not a problem in need of a cure. In fact, intro/extroversion is distributed normally among the general population, just like IQ. Simply put, too much contact with people wears out the introverts, whereas extroverts get energy from social interplay. Only at either extreme do we diagnose psychological disturbance. Shy extroverts are greatly pained by their inability to make friends, while shy introverts don't care so much.

So, find out first whether your daughter is a natural introvert. If she is, encourage her to be successful in her own way, even if that's more in the company of herself than others. But if she's shy and wants to make more friends, you'll want to do some social skills training and, if the situation is severe enough to warrant an anxiety diagnosis, medication management. Shy kids are tough to engage (because they're shy), but some therapists can get past that and tailor a plan specific to the child. That may take some shopping however, because your daughter is likely to be ultra-picky about whom she opens up to.

Adolescence is particularly difficult for introverts, because the group mean (average) shifts toward extroversion, before returning to normal in young adulthood. This leaves very introverted teens feeling even more alone, because there are fewer of them. The best option is to try and find one or two good, shy friends, and then not worry about the rest of the crowd. True introverts will be happiest in those situations and their temperament should be honored, not misunderstood as dysfunctional.

And to make matters more complicated, kids usually can't tell us whether they are shy or introverted. So, before taking any action, I suggest that you interview the school counselor and teachers to gather data, and maybe attend a couple sessions with a licensed kid therapist. As Ben says, there's a limit on what you can do here, so you want to move carefully and select your target behaviors wisely.

Getting Shy Teens Out

Dear Dr. Wes and John,

Your article discussing the benefits of social networking was, in my opinion, right on target. However, the problem is how do parents of introverted shy children get them out of the house and into the world. As a parent of some shy children, I would love some tips on how to get them to overcome their uncomfortable feelings about the world. Keep writing, I will keep reading.

Dr. Wes: There are basically two kinds of "shy" teens and it helps to figure out which category your kids fall into.

The first group includes extroverts who would really like to have more friends but lack social skills. Starting from a young age, they tend to say and do the wrong things at every turn, causing others to become less and less interested in befriending them. The research tells us that it takes classmates less than a day to pick out these kids and to respond to them accordingly, and the response isn't usually very nice.

Some have learning disabilities, Asperger's Syndrome or other developmental delays, or ADHD. Some are gifted intellectually but not socially. After a number of unpleasant social interactions, many decide it's too hard and become increasingly reclusive, essentially giving up on social interplay. Later in adolescence they may tend to congregate with other kids who don't have well-honed social skills and don't expect others to have them either.

Parents, teachers, and therapists find it challenging to work with these kids because these children often struggle with the core elements of change—dialog, coaching, and guidance—all of which are social behaviors. They either can't follow advice or they don't see the need to. The ideal treatment is to place them in some form of supported play or, when they are older, have adults and teen friends coach them to clarify and correct their social errors. Church youth groups that practice tolerance of psychological issues may be ideal, though you really need to shop carefully to be sure that the fit is a good one. All this attention is labor-intensive for parents, but the long-term payoff is worth the effort.

The quickest way to overcome shyness is through a public speaking activity such as debate or theater.

The second group includes kids with various levels of anxiety ranging from fear of public speaking or performance to an inability to go to school, or sometimes even leave the house. These kids might like to have more friends, but making them is such a fearful experience that they don't even get out there and try. This one sounds more like your kids. Unlike the first group, they'll do pretty well after establishing relationships. People like them and enjoy their company. It's getting them past the introduction and relationship development that's difficult. This actually gets harder as they get older because, if you haven't noticed already, teen culture is generally less inclusive than that of childhood and even less tolerant of differences. You also have to work with them in maintaining their relationships, not because other kids shun them, but because they may be so self-conscious that they worry incessantly about having said something wrong to a friend or having embarrassed themselves without knowing it.

Parents should help young teens protect friendships developed in earlier years through sports, church, or school. For the anxious kids, rebuilding lost friendships is a daunting task.

John Murray: My previous column centered on what teens can do to make more friends. Trying to get a resistant teen to make friends is a bit more challenging. You can point and prod your children in the right direction, but they're the ones who must make the leap.

If you haven't already done so, suggest your kids join a club. Whether it's swimming, bowling, or dance, any club will help them interact with others and find friends with similar interests. The quickest way to overcome shyness is through a public speaking activity such as debate or theater. Performing in front of crowds is terrifying at first, yet I've seen the experience transform many teens who only joined because their parents coerced them, but then voluntarily continued the following year. I could barely carry a conversation before I joined theater, but within a year I was bustling with confidence and had made buckets of friends.

Alternatively, you can bring friends to your kids. A common myth held by teens is that you can only "hang out" with people you already know. Actually, sharing experiences with people you don't know is a great way to break the ice. Keep reminding your daughters of potential friends and events, and they'll get the hint. You can even offer to help them throw a party. The process can be exhausting, but it teaches them about the dynamics of how people interact, and gives you a chance to observe them with friends. Remember that there are a lot of other shy children who want someone to spend time with. They just need to be found.

Most importantly, support your children. Teens are wary about talking to people who might reject their friendship. A supportive parent can soften this risk. Talk to them about their social life, and make sure they have another adult to speak with. This is especially important if your teen falls into the first category of shyness Wes mentioned. Even if we don't admit it, we teenagers want to be understood by our parents. Discussing our insecurities can help us move past them.

Victim or Offender

Dear Dr. Wes and Kelly,

Our thirteen-year-old son is exhibiting an emotional pattern of rejecting friends at home and at school. He has a victim mentality about how people don't like him, but my husband and I have observed repeatedly how *he* sabotages his friendships. Any thoughts?

Dr. Wes: To determine whether your son is a victim or offender in situations like this requires him to accurately perceive reality, then accurately convey that to you so you can accurately respond to it. That's an awful lot of accuracy for any thirteen-year-old boy and it may be too much for your son. At the moderate to severe level, these situations tend to involve developmental delays that become more apparent during major transitions like entering middle school. Put on your detective cap and start looking for clues.

When did you first start noticing this pattern? Were there signs of it early in life or did it change as he went through puberty? Did he always

Once you open his life up for discussion, he may believe that you too are against him, only furthering his victim complex.

seem to have problems perceiving things the way others did, TV, movies, the behavior of other kids, instructions you or a teacher gave him, etc.? Did he ever really "get" other kids? Did they "get" him? Did he always have a chip on his shoulder? Did he make friends or mostly stick with the old crowd? Has that old crowd changed in interests, behavior, or attitude? Is he more of an introvert by nature? In adolescence even the introverts tend to shift toward extroversion and sometimes that's a difficult transition.

How does his sabotaging impact the behavior of others? Is there any secondary gain from his behavior, such as receiving more attention from you or manipulating his friends? Do his friends try to pull him in or just cut him off? Does he actually realize in advance that he's likely to lose the friend or does he expect unwavering tolerance? Does losing a friend worry him or is he callous to the loss? These answers give you an outline for beginning to understand how he perceives his interactions with the outside world.

Don't count this as a 400-word workshop on teen diagnosis, but what you're trying to sort out here is whether your son's behavior is driven by anxiety, inattention, developmental delay or perceptual inaccuracy. These tend to reveal themselves in the form of cognitive distortions—things he believes that are not aligned with accepted reality. So, if he's constantly obsessing on what others are thinking of him, he'll tend toward the anxious end of the spectrum. If he impulsively reacts to other people's behavior without adequate reflection, that's an inattentive response, and if he persistently misstates what they do or say, that's a perceptual deficit.

If you can get a read on this, kindly offer to coach him on how to make better decisions. The anxious people respond best to these suggestions because they just care so much. The inattentive people are resistant because they don't care enough. Those with perceptual problems don't really understand what you're talking about and may be offended that you'd even offer.

If you're persistent, you may be able to point out more effective ways for your son to respond. If he refuses to buy-in after a few weeks of this, it may be time to head to a therapist who can help you forge a connection between you and your son and allow him to take direction and modify his behavior. This is admittedly more difficult than it might sound, but it will at least get you started in the right direction.

Kelly Kelin: All parents have a vision of how their children will be when they grow up. Once they actually get there, however, it's surprising to see how far they've strayed from that idealized life. Parents want their children to live normal lives with normal friends, and have a normal school life. But this picture perfect scenario can easily be shattered by behavioral problems.

It's unfortunate that your son has been socially sabotaging himself. While I don't know his complete history, it's highly unlikely that he has developed this mentality out of the blue. Have there been any other problems at school? Has he exhibited any other unusual behaviors? The fact that he takes a victim mentality suggests deeper roots to his problems, like low self-esteem, which would lead him toward becoming a very negative individual. If you don't stem his behavioral patterns now, he may grow up and continue down this path.

First, sit down and talk to your son. Perhaps he really does see the situation differently than you do. For him, life may be emotionally challenging. Next, visit his school and talk to his teachers, principal, counselors, etc. If they see him exhibiting this same negative behavior, set up an appointment with the school counselor for your child. Sometimes it's easier for children to talk to others about their problems rather than talking directly to their parents.

It is important, however, not to be too forceful in this delicate situation. Once you open his life up for discussion, he may believe that you too are against him, only furthering his victim complex.

8 TEEN TECH

Generation Geek

Dr. Wes: A few weeks ago we discussed how to introduce cell phones to pre- or early teens. While planning another article in that series, I had occasion to spend time with my son on the computer. He told me that we needed to go to a certain gaming site, explaining that he'd seen it on Cartoon Network. He described his understanding of how the game worked and asked me to add it to his favorites folder. I suggested that before he was allowed to play he had to show Granny one more time how to navigate her online banking by clicking on the blue underlined links with her mouse. He reluctantly agreed.

Granny is 83. My son is five.

His disproportionate share of computer knowledge reminds me that where technology is concerned, we cannot wait until our kids reach the teen years to begin its introduction and management. Computers and video games are not like cell phones nor even iPods. The perfection of point and click technology makes it possible for any child who has sufficient coordination to tap a mouse or track pad and make just about any dream come true.

Back in my youth, the great Satan was TV, the "boob tube" sitting in the living room, spewing out a vast wasteland of mind-numbing crap to unwitting kids, interspersed with ads for cheap toys and sugary cereal. Parents were warned about the dangers of this electronic babysitter. The government created PBS and "family viewing time" for networks in the early evening, with little real impact.

Kids still watch TV, and the array of kids shows and networks has increased in size and quality. But today's big mind-benders are clearly the computer and the video game console. Unfortunately, this technology often leads to a kind of Faustian bargain between kids and parents wherein these gizmos are used to occupy kids while parents carry out their busy lives. On their end, kids are entranced with these technologies in ways that go beyond my reckoning. I spent a lot of my youth shooting Space Invaders, Asteroids, and pinball bumpers, but never with that much fervor.

> *No one has been arrested for child abuse because they set a passcode on Xbox.*

If you lose control of technology early on, it's incredibly hard to get it back, so it's never too early to make your plan. With kids under eight, introduce video and computer games using a dessert analogy. After we've gotten done the important things of the day—like exercise, learning, rest, and family activities—games are a way to have fun for a little while. Just as we don't eat the whole cake after dinner, we don't play video games for six hours a day.

Sleep is the most crucial activity that we neglect as teens and adults. Because of their intense, exciting, and thought-provoking design, video games are no good before bed. Require children and teens to have an hour of buffer time between the end of gaming and sleep. Sometimes it's useful to sandwich game time, so kids play right after school when they need some non-academic down time. Then they eat dinner, do homework, play outside, etc. Then they game for an hour to ninety minutes before the buffer kicks in.

Creating these habits well before the teen years is critically important and, as with everything else in parenting, a thousand times easier than waiting until problems arise. And when they do, don't be afraid to box the system or lock out the games on the computer.

No one has been arrested for child abuse because they set a passcode on Xbox.

Kelly Kelin: Society has become overwhelmed with the advancement of technology. Companies market new products for our viewing pleasure to nearly every age group, making their impact almost limitless.

We've set no boundary or age limit on technology, making it readily available to anyone who can afford it.

For parents, raising children in a society where materialism is the core value can be quite difficult. If one child gets a cell phone or computer, practically the whole school will have one by the end of the week. But when do you say enough is enough? When you notice your children's social skills have deteriorated because they are too enthralled with their new video game? Or perhaps their joy in life depends on how big the present is?

My generation is known for investing in the latest technology craze and we should be thankful for how many opportunities it has opened up for us. On the other hand, not many people realize how overly attached we've become to these inanimate objects. If we happen to break or lose a cell phone or computer, all hell breaks loose. Our lives have become far too dependent on the conveniences of technology. It's time we move away from that. I understand parents wanting the best for their children. Yet, you can give your children so much more without having to put a dent in your wallet.

As Wes suggests, if you do provide your kids with these technologies, be sure to set up a structure and routine, beginning at an early age. If watching TV, playing video games, or clicking on the computer consumes most of their time, be sure to provide them with alternatives. There are plenty of outdoor activities worth their time. Require some social time, or have them walk the dog to keep them busy and away from the technology for awhile. Technology can be a part of your child's life, but that doesn't mean it has to rule it.

Tracking Teens

Dr. Wes: Last year, Marissa and I did a column on new methods of surveillance that integrate into anything, especially cars and cell phones. They allow parents to know everything from where their kids are to how fast they're driving. This equipment is now being mass-marketed, joining a growing number of high tech solutions for 21st century supervision. These include:

- Spyware to filter everything teens do online and to (supposedly) prevent them from doing it.
- History logs for mail, text message, online, and cell phone.

- Home security systems installed as much to keep teens in as to keep intruders out.
- Camera phones allowing parents to verify whether their teens are actually where they say they are.
- Breathalyzers and home drug testing.

Whether you consider any of these a blessing or a curse depends squarely upon how you view teen culture and parental responsibility. Either way, these methods are here to stay and will only become cheaper and easier to use. As always, our ethics lag far behind.

When considering this issue, keep in mind the core tension here: The right of young people to exercise reasonable freedom versus the right of parents to exercise reasonable oversight. In this, there is nothing new. These methods only extend old-school snooping practices (reading a teen's diary, going through his room, receiving a friendly tip from the neighbors, forming a parent network, etc.).

So, the real ethical issue isn't the method, but rather the balance that should be struck between kids' rights and parents' rights. Parents have always had to decide how much to restrain their children's overdeveloped yearning for freedom and underdeveloped skill at independence. This is pretty much the point of parenting adolescents. That's why there are so many billboards encouraging parents to know where their kids are and what they're up to. Any movement toward extreme control or naïve trust can prevent the child learning from natural and logical consequence or, conversely, from getting into serious and irreversible trouble.

One of the purposes of parents is to teach kids that rights are limited and all privileges come with responsibility.

We also have to consider these new solutions against a backdrop of equally dramatic changes in our culture. Since the sixties, there has actually been a tremendous increase in teen self-determination. Whether they're "good" or "bad," these technologies are only marketable because they address parental concerns about that generational change in teen freedom. Parents must consider all these issues *before* they get involved in tracking or surveilling their teen.

This may well be the most important teen-parent issue of our generation and now would be a good time to begin discussing it.

John Murray: Oh, the wonders of this day and age! While the ability to constantly know a child's location may sound pleasing to some parents, others wonder if GPS has gone too far.

In the security versus liberty debate, I'm Big Brother's big brother. While some might complain about the threat to privacy posed by geopositioning, I see traveling outside the house as a privilege, not a right. As such, parents are licensed to place restrictions on it. In order to travel in the first place, parents must trust their offspring to obey house rules and travel safely. I assume that if a parent were using GPS to monitor their teen, it would be because they were concerned their child would travel to an unauthorized zone. But if a teen needs GPS to keep him in line, it's hard to justify letting him travel in the first place.

At a few hundred bucks, this technology does not come cheap and, like any technology, teenagers will be able to manipulate it. Remember who helped you install the parental controls on the family computer? I am confident that my generation will quickly discover a straightforward method to render these technologies useless.

GPS tracking might be okay if used purely as a safety instrument, and not as a means to enforce rules. For example, if a teen was going on a camping trip, GPS could help parents find him if he gets lost. But even so, there are more practical tools like cell phones that could serve that end.

One of the purposes of parents is to teach kids that rights are limited and all privileges come with responsibility. To this end, geotracking is counter-productive because it allows teens to have a privilege (traveling) without fulfilling their responsibility (proving they will follow the rules). When they leave for college, this level of supervision will be impossible and new young adults will have nothing but their consciences to guide them. Parents looking to protect their children should give this gadget a pass and look to more traditional methods of monitoring.

I ♥ My Cell Phone

Dr. Wes: Most of us—those old enough to have teenage children—remember when the epitome of adolescence was a phone that seemed to grow out of a child's ear around the time he or she turned thirteen. That phone was connected to a cord, or later a radio signal from handset to base, which made it easier for parents to turn it off at will.

Most of us had "phone curfews," which we bravely struggled to violate. Since everyone in the family relied on a single wire coming into a home, parents could listen in and enforce the rules. It's hard to believe now, but affordable cell phone service for teens only emerged about twelve years ago. Texting came to prominence in the middle of the decade, and Internet-equipped smartphones are even newer.

Once telephones became individualized personal communication devices, many parents slackened the old rules with which they themselves had grown up. Below, Miranda shares a great list of no-fly zones that should be discussed on the day you activate your ten-year-old's service, so I'll just hit my number one rule. Just home from training at the American Psychological Association, I am again reminded of the chronic level of sleep deprivation in this country, especially among teens. A chief reason is that many kids nowadays unrepentantly sleep *with* their phones.

From day one, phones should be on chargers at night, kept safely in the parents' bedroom. By the way, you'll want to turn off the sound, because your teen's friends will still send texts throughout the night, which just reminds us of how many parents need to get on board with this radical idea from back in 1977.

Miranda Davis: I admit I love my cell phone. My generation has been raised to feel most comfortable when communicating through technology, and parents enjoy the safety net of being in constant communication with their children. There are times, however, when it's nothing more than a problem glued to my hand. Here are a few places where cell phones should be out of sight.

School. Don't you hate it when someone isn't listening to your fascinating story because she's texting or tweeting? That's how teachers feel when you're on the phone during a lecture. We all know that school isn't supposed to be enjoyable, but who are you texting that isn't already there with you?

Public Places. Have you ever seen one of those people screaming into his phone at the grocery store or while sitting at a nice restaurant? If you're somewhere and your phone rings, politely excuse yourself and go outside.

Family Time. If your parents haven't nagged you to put away your phone yet, you're a unicorn among your fellow teens. Leave it out of your family dinners, game night, visiting relatives and religious services.

Your parents love you and want to spend time with you. If that isn't reason enough, then remember this: they pay the bill and have the ability to disconnect your contact with the outside world.

Date Night. When you're out with a significant other, don't text your friends. Whether you've been on two dates or two hundred, a relationship can't grow if you're more concerned with Facebook than the present conversation.

Work. Even if you just work part-time because your parents made you, don't text on the job. I leave my phone in my car at work to keep me from temptation. You'll need to use that job for a recommendation someday and such professional behavior will show just how mature you are.

Fear of Social Networking

Dr. Wes: Headline: Online predators are stalking your child. Hundreds of dangerous goons have been nabbed by sting operations in which officers pose as teenagers willing to engage in sex. *Dateline* runs a version of this sting all the time. Parents, schools, and law enforcement urge kids to avoid online social networks as perfect dens for predators to seek out hapless victims. As John notes below, even Congress has gotten involved.

When I first heard this, I was instantly suspicious. There are many serious issues facing today's teens. This did not seem like one of them.

First of all, real sex offenders are crafty and devious people, sometimes victimizing many children. Those *Dateline* guys don't exactly match this description. I called a Kansas City radio show recently and asked an FBI sting agent how many real victims his targets had harmed. He admitted the FBI had no idea. I suspect it's close to zero because real sex offenders wouldn't fall for such a silly trick. Moreover, with a few notable exceptions, the idea of teenagers soliciting or responding to adult sexual advances online seemed unlikely to me. Over the years, thousands of kids have shared some pretty shocking secrets about their sexual practices. Only one or two men-

Let's not fool ourselves. Real sex offenders are everywhere. The only real defense is to raise wise, self-protective kids.

tioned this one. Most were instead harmed by family members and trusted adults. Not some creepy dude on the Internet.

Media scares are nothing new. In the 1980s, we were told of "nursery school sex rings" forming complex networks all around the country. In the late 1970s, complex networks of cults supposedly sacrificed hundreds of people (and cattle) in the name of Satan. Yet, both of these threats were disproven, and I've long suspected the same thing for the online predator frenzy.

In fact, we now have some data to prove it. The National Center for Missing and Exploited Children, the leading experts on such matters, just issued a study of 55,000 households. They found that teenagers are actually receiving *fewer* sexual solicitations despite an enormous increase in Internet access. The authors credit the teens themselves, noting they are becoming "Smarter about where they hang out and with whom they communicate online." Of the sexual solicitations that were reported, many "came from other teens rather than adults, and few rose to the level of predation." The report adds, "A significant portion of what [teens] are calling sexual solicitation is merely teens being teens…the dangers are real but they are not as significant as they have been hyped in recent months… People have fears that these crimes involve offenders and predators who look at these sites and then seek to identify these kids. That's not really what's going on."

If reasonable safety precautions are followed, networking sites allow access to friendship, which is especially valuable for those young people less socially adept than their peers. Kids can make friends all over the world or right down the street. While that shouldn't replace "real world" friends, it can help build relationships in a way that has never existed before.

Let's not fool ourselves. Real sex offenders are everywhere. Most are undiscovered. They integrate into our communities, our families, and daily life. The only real defense is to raise wise, self-protective kids, as John notes below. Besides, if you think about it, it's safer to sit at home and block an email address that you don't approve of, than to go to the mall and confront a creeper in real life.

John Murray: Not that you had anything to fear anyway. Our civil servants are working hard to pass a new law to protect your children (That's your cue to panic). The Deleting Online Predators Act, sponsored by U.S. Rep. Michael Fitzpatrick, R-Ohio, would require minors to receive parental consent before visiting social networks on public school and library computers. Remember when Republicans stood for less regulation? One has to wonder why Congress felt more qualified to decide where students should surf than the schools and libraries themselves.

Personal websites have their place, but one has to appreciate the risks involved. The public may be overreacting to online sex predators, but it's not paying nearly enough attention to the concept of "digital dirt." About a year ago, a university professor announced he was going to teach a class on intelligent design. Some said he would not approach the topic objectively, but he dismissed the claim as unfounded. Then came the discovery of comments on a listserv for The Society of Open Minded Atheists and Agnostics that proved otherwise. The class was cancelled, and he resigned as department chair.

Even a university professor can forget the first law of Internet safety. Never post what you do not want on the front page of *The New York Times*. Teens would be wise to learn from his example and design a Facebook they'd be comfortable with their bosses seeing.

If you ever choose to meet an online acquaintance, the usual litany of precautions apply. Make sure your friends are real, and not salespeople (such as ForBiddeN, a luscious young mistress who doubles as an advertiser for Axe.). Always meet in a public place, preferably with a buddy. Be sure a parent knows what you have planned. If you have to hide your new friend, you probably shouldn't be meeting up. Finally, having a constructive activity planned will go a long way to keep you out of trouble, giving you more time to write Congress.

Real Internet Foibles

Dr. Wes: I saw my first PC in 1978. I was fifteen and, like any teen, I quickly put it to its best possible use. I wrote a little program that printed on the screen, "Hi, Wes. I'm the Radio Shack TRS-80." It was amazing. Technology has changed a bit in thirty years, but teens are still trying to put computers to their best possible use. Except now when you write a program to say "Hi," someone 12,000 miles away can respond.

It's still amazing.

Unfortunately, technology nearly always outpaces good judgment. Nowhere is this more apparent than in teens' relationships with the

Internet. I've commented that the web is a far safer place to hang out with friends than the real world, but I've come to believe that parents must get a better grip on technology in order to make kids safe and successful consumers.

While one may feel better with Cyber Nanny on the box, in reality there's no way to keep teens isolated from Internet problems. Instead, you must rely on a decidedly low-tech solution—one-to-one communication to apply *values and ethics* to a teen Internet user.

First, we must accept that kids are active participants rather than simply victims of the Internet. Nothing on the web comes blasting out of the wall and down your Ethernet cable without some assistance. Even the nastiest spams require a response by the reader. Every case I've seen of bad Internet experiences has included a healthy dose of being in the wrong virtual place, doing the wrong virtual things, at the wrong time. Thus, teaching kids how to be safe online, or in the real world for that matter, requires less focus on offenders and more on what attracts our children to the places we don't want them to go.

Parents need to discuss Internet posting with their children both from a defensive standpoint, and an ethical one.

To get started, here's our list of Internet foibles. If any of them are out of your awareness as a parent, spend some time catching up, because they are not out of your teen's awareness.

Pornography. I'm no prude, but I am astonished when a parent challenges me to surf what's available online, usually after they've caught their child viewing something disturbing. Things have really changed. I'm not going into detail here, but the amount and "diversity" of what is available at no charge is really beyond reason. Back in the day, psychologists assured parents that kids sneaking a dirty magazine or book wasn't necessarily harmful and should not be punished with shame and guilt. I can no longer give that advice, because so much of online pornography is, by any standard, violent and degrading, all right there for anyone to peruse.

My biggest concern is that these images portray sexual acts in a way that is counter-educational, teaching kids the wrong manner, attitude, and method of sexuality. That's about as helpful as a drunk driver teaching driver's ed. The short answer to this problem is to beat the Internet to the punch. Have open discussions with preteens about sex.

Make it a natural and healthy topic and always within the context of some value system. The more we make sex seem perverse or uncomfortable, the more we redirect kids toward the perverse and uncomfortable files on the Internet, which then become our sex-ed teachers. **Privacy and Human Rights.** Modern teens have a different sense of privacy for themselves and others. We all realize that teens tend to act before they think. That's been true forever. What's new is the ability to capture these actions on video, text messaging, IM, and email and then to distribute them to a worldwide audience with a few mouse clicks. If there's one huge downside of the Internet, this is it. Parents need to discuss online posting with their children both from a defensive standpoint, and an ethical one. Teach what is right and wrong online, just as we suggest with sex and drugs, and how to avoid being a victim or an offender. Online, it's all too easy to end up as one or both.

John Murray: I have two pet Internet peeves on my list:

Respect Intellectual Property. I hope most teenagers would not swipe a DVD from a store, but ripping off intellectual property is equally harmful. Books, movies, video games, and albums require tremendous investments in human capital. If the investment is not recouped, people will stop making good material. In some cases, TV shows have been cancelled when pirates made their material available online. In America alone, movie pirates have been responsible for loss of 141,000 jobs and 20.5 billion dollars of industrial output.

Equally distressing is the trend of students copying essays from the Internet to turn in as their own. While all the statements about intellectual property apply here, one must also remember that it's actually more difficult to get away with plagiarism than it used to be. Anti-plagiarism software is making huge strides, and teachers can usually tell when the tone of a work is not that of their student. Students who get caught are often punished with failing grades, while those who don't may go on to commit bigger acts of dishonesty. Colleges and employers are much less forgiving.

Use in Moderation. Although Internet addiction is not formally recognized as a disorder, it is easy to be sucked up in the vast array of amusements available online. Not only can this lead to time management problems, but also to a single-minded view of what is available in the larger world. Many of my peers use the Internet exclusively when doing research, forgetting to investigate material available in print.

The Internet is an astonishing tool, but like all good things, it must be used wisely.

Reading Your Teen's Media

Dear Dr. Wes and Samantha,

Is it OK to read my daughter's text messages without her knowledge? Do parents have the right to ask for access to Facebook accounts?

Samantha Schwartz: Parents have the right to see their children's Facebook accounts and text messages. Parents usually pay for their children's phones, computers, and Internet access, so they have a right to access them. It's a parent's job to keep teens safe, and checking online activity is part of that job.

I'm not saying parents should make a new hobby of creeping around their teens' Facebook pages. If they haven't broken the rules before, parents have no reason to secretly check out their teens' Facebook profiles or text messages, and they shouldn't need to ask for their passwords and read their conversations. Instead, they should just ask their teens who they are chatting with and what they are chatting about. They should also feel free to look over their teens' shoulders from time to time. Parents should try to be umbrellas, sheltering their kids from bad elements when needed.

As a general rule, laptops and computers should be kept in a common area of the home so parents can better monitor their use. Also, disable all built-in webcams if possible. Hackers can turn on a webcam and watch computer users at any time. If the computer has a webcam and it can't be disabled, put a sticker over the lens when your teen isn't using it.

If your teen has already broken your rules, asking for her Facebook password is reasonable. Checking her Facebook and texts about twice a week will help you keep track of what she's up to. Remember to check her inbox, not just her profile page. That's the most likely place where secret transactions would take place. When she proves herself more trustworthy, you can give her more privacy.

Dr. Wes: It's never too late to start a good habit or eliminate a bad one. But this topic demands some serious upfront planning, early intervention, and as little deception as possible. The key word is "proactive" and I don't mean the acne cleanser. By now, we've all had enough experience with the Internet and cell phones to understand how they work. There's no excuse to be caught off guard by technologies that dramatically change our children's lives.

Let's be clear. These particular technologies represent a purposeful and deliberate violation of personal privacy by the user. In fact, research suggests a significant shift in how teens view privacy now that their lives are out there for all the world to see. But who needs research? Just review a few teen texts or postings that include rampant substance abuse references (with pix) and X-rated discussions of sexual exploits (with pix) to see what I mean.

So, who's excluded from this exposé of everything teens think, do, or say? Parents. Kids don't want us to read the material that will be viewed and *never ever* erased from servers around the world, even if the account is closed. And, because it's considered private, one to one texting is even more dicey. When you text someone you're creating a transcript, which takes exactly five seconds to forward (with pix) to anyone with a cell phone. So much for "private" communication.

Do not wait to set these rules until your child receives the first sext-message, posts a provocative pose on Facebook, or cuts a drug deal online. Proactive parents start when their kids first connect to Cartoon Network, Disney.com, Club Penguin, etc. They set boundaries, define the Internet as open-access (everything you see I can see too), discuss ethical obligations, harm to self and others, and so on.

The best adage on this comes from Spiderman, and for true geeks, the warning at the UNIX terminal prompt: "With great power, comes great responsibility." Repeat this mantra over and over from the first day your kids touch a keyboard and mouse.

None of this will halt the progress of hormones, curiosity, and questionable judgment. But when your child does start getting into trouble online or with her phone, you'll be in a stronger position to intervene, not just react to the crisis.

Hope for the best and plan for the worst. That one predates Spiderman and UNIX.

Facebook Privacy…Not

Dear Dr. Wes and Samantha,

I've read your articles about social networking, but I have a ten-year-old daughter and I feel like if she is given no privacy and no trust (I read your comment on that also) she will move heaven and earth to break every rule I give her. But I don't want her getting in trouble online. She has Facebook and MySpace accounts and email and is happy to tell me the passwords. However, where do you draw the line?

Dr. Wes: First off, the words "privacy" and "Facebook" should never be used in the same sentence. Yet I hear this all the time, from kids wanting electronic "privacy" and parents worried about giving it to them.

As teenagers get older, they must receive greater latitude in what they're allowed to keep private. That's not because growth and maturity make them more trustworthy. That won't happen until they're well past the age of majority. Some teens have better judgment than others, but even the wisest kids don't want you knowing everything they do, because you probably wouldn't (and shouldn't) approve. Instead, you must respect privacy more as they age because they need to experience a reasonable degree of trial and error, and the consequences therein. Besides, you can't follow a seventeen-year-old around 24/7 unless you have really grave concerns about his or her conduct.

The point of being a teen is to do teenager things. The point of being a parent is to do parent things.

The entire point of social networking is to *post online whatever you want the world to see.* Granted, that world is supposed to be limited to your "Friends" list, but that's like saying articles in *USAToday* can only be read by subscribers. Once it's posted, it's up there and it will never go away, which leaves us with the big question: If you're child wants to put her life online, why wouldn't she want you to see it? Is it really that smart for a teen, or even a young adult, to post content they don't want their mom to see? What about a future employer or perfect dating partner?

Besides, your child isn't even a teenager yet. While it *may* be arguable whether a sixteen or seventeen-year-old must "friend" her mom and dad, anyone younger should not be allowed free reign of Facebook. As we've discussed, the immediate threat is not from a bunch of pervs in cyberspace. It's from material and activity kids get straight from their peer group and what they put up themselves. So, especially at this early stage, it is imperative that you supervise her online activity closely. As she gets older, you can review those constraints to see if they are still age appropriate.

Remember, the point of being a teen is to do teenager things. The point of being a parent is to do parent things. Pick your battles carefully, but set an age-appropriate structure for your child's use of technology. Don't get caught in the trap of trusting kids in ways they simply can't handle. Good online habits between you and your ten-year-old now will pay off later when things get a lot rockier, which they will.

Samantha Schwartz: As Wes notes, age ten is pretty young to join Facebook and MySpace, so you really need to watch out for her. It's okay to set limits. She's only a child. If she's a bit of a rule breaker and doesn't respond well to being told what to do, you'll need some new approaches to the problem. Try these:

Scare her. Remind her she's a ten-year-old on websites that anyone from eight to eighty could be using. Tell her that there are scary people online who pretend they are older or younger than they really are because they are trying to hurt her or make her do things she doesn't want to do. Explain to her that unless she knows the person in real life, there is no way to know whether he/she is safe. Find a story about a girl around her age who got into a really bad situation. Read the story with her, and tell her it could happen to anyone, and you just want to make sure it doesn't happen to her.

Look at her profile while she's using it. Make a habit of being in the room while she's on the Internet. Don't let her take a laptop to her room. It's easier to be involved in her Internet usage if you take genuine interest in the site. Help her pick out a profile image (maybe have her use an image of a favorite character on TV, a baby picture, or a picture of her with lots of friends so she's not as recognizable) and a background color. Help her write her info box so you can limit personal information. Ask her to show you all her friends, and casually inquire about how she knows each of them. If she sees that you care what she's putting up, she's more likely to think it through the next time she posts something.

Give her some privacy, but not total privacy. Use her password to get onto her account periodically and check her private messages. These are the most dangerous and hidden parts of social networking sites. Don't read her messages with friends or other people you've heard her talk about. However, if you see a name that looks suspicious, read the message.

Protect your daughter by setting limits for her that she understands. Answer all her questions about rules you make, and she'll feel less inclined to break them. Her safety is much more important than her privacy or her liking you.

Naked Pictures

Dear Dr. Wes and Julia,

My husband and I were horrified to learn that pictures of our daughter's naked body were recently sent to half the kids in her school by a former boyfriend (or so we think). You can't see her face, but let's just say there aren't any questions about who it is. When we confronted her, she was less embarrassed than we were, which was even more disturbing. She was more upset that we found out than the fact that it happened. She said she had trusted this guy and let him have the pictures she'd taken with her digital camera. Then they broke up and the rest is (bad) history. I'm not sure whether this is a question or a warning to other parents, but I wish you'd find time to respond to it.

Dr. Wes: Oh yes we will. This is going on a lot nowadays, so consider yourself unwitting pioneers into a whole new world. Vanessa Hudgins of *High School Musical* fame nearly lost her career for doing exactly the same thing as your daughter. The explosion of digital photography has yielded both good and bad. Your case illustrates the bad.

Young people find it interesting and rather daring to explore their bodies with digital photography. Yet, in doing so, they create images that can intentionally or accidentally get shared. Then, as your daughter learned, agreements to keep them private evaporate when relationships deteriorate. For teens, I strongly suggest learning to use the delete button after any such explorations; *never,* under any circumstances, let the microchip come out of hiding; *do not* send the photos to anyone; and *never* post them online, even if you have a "private" webpage.

Young people have also been recording their sexual exploits on video, with or without permission from their partners. I suggest that if anyone is so victimized, they take legal action. Unfortunately, embarrassment often gets in the way and offenders aren't punished. And before participating willingly in such photo shoots, think very carefully about the long-term consequences. None of them are good.

Keep in mind that the teen who takes a nude photo may not intend to be stupid, but only to signify a mature relationship.

Teens also chat away on text messaging and instant messenger, forgetting that every single word is archived on someone else's computer, which can then be used maliciously if friendships turn sour and alliances shift. And finally, there's good old MySpace and Facebook. There was an old show called "Kids Say the Darndest Things" that took advantage of preteens' inability to censor themselves. I fear that during the TV writer's strike someone will come up with a new show called "Teens Post the Darndest Things." It won't be pretty.

Thankfully, most of our own teen indiscretions are long forgotten. Today, they're often preserved for everyone to see…*forever.*

Julia Davidson: Taking naked pictures seems to be the "it" thing now. Giving them to your partner symbolizes trust, intimacy and a very adult relationship…not. The only thing that a naked picture demonstrates is your comfort in front of a digital camera. For female participants, these pictures reinforce the idea that a woman's body is an object to be ogled. I don't mean to slam an intimate gift exchanged between partners, but there are so many better ways to show your love than with a risqué snapshot. To entrust a naked picture to anybody is to sign away your privacy and commonsense.

A naked photo may seem like the ultimate show of trust and adoration, but kids are not XXX porn stars, and they wouldn't like to be labeled as such. Relationships between teenagers are so unpredictable. You don't know how fast a picture of you can end up in someone else's hands. Chances are, they will. Let's imagine the person you give your photo to. Now imagine that person morphing into a middle-aged adult; your sibling; or worst of all, your parents or grandparents.

Parents have every right to be enraged or confused about the naked photo epidemic. Keep in mind, though, that the teen who takes a nude photo may not intend to be stupid, but only to signify a mature relationship. It's alarming when it's your daughter, but understand she's just trying to act more mature than she is. No teenager wants their relationship to be denounced as "puppy love." Hence, you get teenagers who seem like they're growing up way too quickly and acting older than their age, rather than the innocent cherubs you once knew.

Yes, it is disturbing to find a topless shot of your child circulating the Internet, but it was probably intended as a misguided show of love. Any apathy you perceive from your daughter as a response is likely a cover up for the embarrassment of a sweet gesture gone horribly wrong.

9 FAMILY LIFE

Reasons for Family Strife

Dear Dr. Wes and John,

What do you see as the three top reasons for family strife today?

Dr. Wes: This one made me think, trying to narrow it down to just three factors. I decided to choose the three things I most commonly wish I could go back in time and change about families I've seen over the years. Not incidentally, the stats are with me, and most of these problems have their origin in adolescence when personality and family-style are being honed.

Early or swift coupling followed by premature pregnancy. I realize that sounds like two answers in one, but they tend to go together. Couples who get pregnant before they're prepared to do so are at high risk of family problems down the road. There's really no age barrier on this one. I've seen it among people at any childbearing age. However, the younger the couple is, the more the resulting problems are multiplied. In general, a couple has to be a couple, and work out all the problems therein, before they can be highly successful parents.

Babies don't just need to be wanted, they need to be desperately wanted. An unplanned pregnancy can turn into either a lifelong love or a focal point of resentment and rejection. Of course, I've seen people make the best of this difficult situation and pull it off. I admire and learn from them, precisely because the odds were stacked against them. Among struggling families, this is a very common denominator.

Under-involved parents. Whether they're married, divorced, or never married at all, families function best when two cooperative parents offer substantial time and attention to their children. We ran an essay on Father's Day this year[12] that illustrated a child's pain when one of her parents goes missing or becomes uninvolved after a divorce. The same can be true for parents who are still married, but don't take active interest in their children. I really respect solo parents (married, single, or divorced) who strive to make up for the lack of a co-parent. However, their children often remain haunted by the thought that they were not good or important enough for the absent parent. And so the workload for the remaining parent more than doubles.

Then there are cases where both parents are too involved in work or other activities to be active in their children's lives. This may become particularly apparent in adolescence when parents errantly feel they've put in their time and can now relax while their kids supervise themselves.

Substance abuse. I've seen families in which an alcoholic or drug abuser held it together well enough not to damage the rest of the family, but these were few and far in between. In general, substance abuse is problematic because it creates an unpredictable, chaotic, and anxiety-ridden environment. It also tends to pass down from parent to child. Peer pressure is not the best predictor of teen substance abuse. Parental use is.

John Murray: Here's my list:
Divorce. The average divorce costs $20,000, not including the increased costs of living afterwards. Ample evidence suggests that divorce is emotionally costly too. Children of divorce are twice as likely to drop out of school, six times as likely to feel alone. Forty nine percent are likely to get divorced as adults. With 53% of marriages ending in divorce today, couples should take steps to avoid this grim future. One way is through premarital counseling, in which couples discuss tough questions about their plans and learn the squishier elements of their future matrimony and careers. Other factors include being engaged for at least six months, living separately until the wedding, and waiting until

---

[12] Reprinted just below this column.

adulthood to tie the knot. Some authors suggest waiting as long as your mid- to late-twenties.

Financial Issues[13]. Money is a staple for all families, and poor financial planning is a major cause of family strife. The average household carries $8,000 in credit card debt and personal savings are at the lowest rate since the Great Depression. When it comes time to pay the bills, some families fight over who is at fault for spending too much. The working parent may wish she earned more, but when she does get a raise, the family simply increases its rate of spending. Instead, families need to work together to develop a realistic budget that includes all the essentials and limits wasteful spending. Financial discipline is difficult at first, but it pays huge dividends once mastered. In their high school and college years, teenagers should learn to balance a budget without resorting to quick fix credit.

Communication. It sounds like a cliché, but poor communication is at the root of many problems facing American families. This week, *Time* magazine reported the average American spends nearly three times as much time watching television as they do socializing. Time constraints aren't the problem here, priorities are. Family members should seek first to understand each other's feelings, then to state their own perspective on important issues. If each member feels their views have been heard and respected, he or she will feel much more comfortable with the final resolution.

Father's Day

Dr. Wes: This week I wanted to run an essay I recently received from a seventh-grade girl. We haven't used Double Take as an outlet for other teen authors, but I felt this piece covered a particularly important topic with Father's Day coming up. It's also very well written. With permission, I have shared it with several clients and each has found it meaningful. I will warn readers that this is not a young girl's sentimental tribute to her dad. It is instead a very real and heartfelt expression of how girls

---

[13] John's insight here is remarkable. *Two years* before the great recession of 2008, he was pointing out substantial flaws in family finance and excess credit, the national extension of which led to the economic downturn. Remember what I wrote in the introduction about just how smart teens are?

need their fathers and how some dads need to take that role more seriously.

Dads, I hope that after honest reflection you cannot find yourself in this girl's words. If you can, I advise you to make this Father's Day one of atonement and renewal. I've seen many men make the serious decision to start over with their kids and succeed splendidly. Being a parent is the most worthy of all vocations.

Essayist: When I was a little girl I used to say, "Oh yeah? Well, my dad can beat up your dad!" I never really thought about it, but I think most kids, besides me, used that phrase, too. I never really thought about those seemingly insignificant quirky sayings, but now I realize how serious we were. Sure, the thought of my dad beating up someone else's dad was funny, but I was proud knowing that he could beat up someone else's dad. I was always proud of my dad, even after he divorced my mother because he had an affair. No matter what my dad did, I was always behind him 100%. Even as I grew into a hormonal preteen, my faith in my father never wavered.

> *The only way we would want space from our dads is if they got overly protective, which, in my opinion, would be better than this aggravating indifference.*

So many girls I know say that they hate their father. Most have divorced parents, live with their mother, and complain that they don't see their father enough; or they live with their father and complain that he doesn't care about them. I am the girl living with my mother, longing for my dad to finally figure out that he is wanted in my life. He thinks that because I'm into guys now, because I wear make-up and bras, I don't want him around. In actuality, those are all the reasons that I do want him around.

All I've ever wanted from my dad is acceptance. I wanted reassurance that I would always be his beautiful princess, no matter what age. I wanted to be recognized as a blossoming young woman, yet also consoled with the knowledge that Dad wasn't scared of my changes in mentality, emotionality, and physicality. That was, and still is, the most important part of my relationship with my father, but only in my dreams. The moment I mention my chest, mascara, or boyfriend, Dad goes berserk, and not outwardly either; I would be happy if he got all scared that I would run out of tampons, but only if he openly showed his concern. The way he hides his embarrassment of my new feminine maturity is frustrating. The least he could do is have one of his friends do an FBI background check on my boyfriend and his family. That would be much better than him just pretending he didn't hear all of the details about my first kiss! I mean, stuff like that is really important to teen girls. In fact, my ultimate dream is for my dad to be one of those sensitive dads who listens to me bashing my ex, or who gladly lets me use him as an emotional punching bag when I'm bummed out. I want him to gossip and buy teen magazines with me, and go to the gas station to get ice cream for me in the middle of the night so I can fulfill my monthly cravings.

I guess that dads can't let themselves be too close with their daughters, in fear of being pushed away, shunned. How can we push you away when we can't even see you? It's like a preemptive strike against our independence. The only way we would want space from our dads is if they got overly protective, which, in my opinion, would be better than this aggravating indifference.

Marissa Ballard: A lot of what the writer says here makes sense. Many teenage girls long for closeness with their dads, but are too shy or proud to really express it. Society doesn't always place a lot of importance on father-daughter relationships, at least not as much as is placed on mothers and daughters.

It should be said, though, that there are many dedicated fathers out there who are doing a wonderful job connecting and befriending their kids. Fathers are very important in their daughters' lives and their role should be appreciated. While mothers can teach their daughters many things, there are some lessons only dads can give.

Happy Father's Day to all dads out there!

Breaking the News

Dear Dr. Wes and Ben,

My husband and I are going to divorce. What's the best way to break the news to our teenagers (thirteen, fifteen, and nineteen)? We want to do the least damage possible.

Dr. Wes: This is one of life's problems that actually has pretty strict and straightforward rules, yet, in their hurt and anguish, far too many divorcing parents violate them all. So, I applaud your concern and appreciate the chance to address this topic.

The first rule is what I call getting the story right. You and your husband need to sit down and agree on: (a) exactly how you want to explain the divorce to your teens; and (b) what you will and will not say outside of those joint discussions. Ben offers some excellent tips on that below, but suffice it to say that the person getting dumped in a marriage often struggles to keep out bitterness in any discussion with the children, while the person doing the dumping has a hard time not moving on too easily and too quickly. Nothing is worse for kids in the early stages of a divorce than hearing how bad one parent is, or how indifferent the other. Remember, the less you say, the less you have to take back, so choose your words wisely.

The next rule is to create order. Kids need to know that regardless of the disaster at hand, their parents have everything under control. The more you sound like you've actually thought all this through, the more easily your teens will adjust. Given their ages, may be tempting to solicit input on parenting time (i.e. where they will be assigned to live at any given moment of the week) from your kids. However, that task is better left to a therapist who can conduct these delicate talks without revealing everything that was said. Find someone specializing in divorce and custody matters, because that area of practice is a whole different ball of wax.

Finally, *do not* use your teens for emotional support. While there may be some tears shed together, you and your spouse should use social or professional support to do your venting and unloading. Your kids need to see you dealing with your own grief and loss in order to deal with theirs, so take out the garbage somewhere else.

Ben Markley: Here's a secret: your kids don't care whose fault it is. If your house burns down, you probably care less about who knocked over the candle and more about where you're going to live.

Your kids don't need or want to know that you think your spouse is irresponsible or a liar or whatever the case may be. The instant you do that, they feel they need to pick a side, and someone is going to be resented. Even worse, if you tell your son that his father is a liar, then he might begin to project that into his own personality. Like father, like son, right? So, those kinds of comments trap your kids in a confusing blame game where nobody wins.

When you tell them about the divorce, do it together. Explain the situation without accusations. They have to know that you're still their parents, that they don't have to choose a bad guy, and that you will both love them, regardless. That is what they care about.

Doesn't Want to Visit Dad

Dear Dr. Wes and Samantha,

As my daughter gets into her mid-teens she is less interested in spending time at her dad's. He moved to the suburbs, and it takes her out of her element and time with friends to go there. He doesn't like it when she brings this up and blames me for putting this idea into her head. But I don't see her acting any differently than any teenager. I'd really rather she just go and keep the peace. So now she's mad at me too.

Samantha Schwartz: You're right. Your daughter *is* just being a teenager. She seems to have no problem with seeing her dad in general. It's the location she has a problem with. Because he chose to move, he's going to have to make some changes in the way he interacts with his daughter if he wants to be greeted with open arms.

It might help if he came to visit her in her hometown more often. It helps to set up a pattern so there are no surprises that force her to reschedule with friends. She and her dad could have a Thursday night dinner date, a Saturday walk in the park, or a Sunday morning coffee shop outing. By including local activities in their repertoire, your ex will show your daughter that he's making an effort to be a part of her world, rather than dragging her out to join his.

When divorce comes into play, we tend to over-read teenage behavior and believe it is related to the divorce rather than normal developmental changes.

However, she still needs to visit her dad in his home and he should work to make this more enjoyable. I have friends with divorced parents who have another set of friends at their second home. Your daughter would feel a lot better about spending time at his house if she had friends there.

There are several ways she can meet people. Your ex-husband could host a neighborhood potluck. Or, if he's intimidated by that, he could ask around about people your daughter's age in his community and help set up a time for them to meet. If at all possible, find an activity or group your daughter can join while visiting him. Being part of a church youth group or community center class will make her feel more connected to his home.

Your daughter will probably not act grateful for these changes at first, and may resist making new friends there because she already has a local group she really likes. Give it a few weeks though. If she still has an attitude, explain to her that her dad is really making an effort. Tell her that she will be going to his house no matter what, so it's now about her choosing to make the most of it.

Dr. Wes: When divorce comes into play, we tend to over-read teenage behavior and believe it is related to the divorce rather than normal developmental changes. Almost every household, married or divorced, has the same set of issues with teens wanting more time with friends and less with parents. The goal is to set a reasonable distribution of that time. After a divorce, it becomes easy to see this kind of behavior as something more malign, like the teen is rejecting the parent rather than growing out of a more dependent childhood phase.

That said, there's a reason many custody evaluators see moving away as a severe impediment to the parent-child relationship. Sometimes a parent will petition the court to move and want to take the child. Judges tend to frown on this for exactly the reasons you're seeing right now. It's very difficult to do what we call "distance parenting," even if you're just forty-five minutes down the road.

Just as Samantha notes, participating in the life of a teenager is not about having her come visit you. It's about getting involved in what she does day-in and day-out. That's why I remain a fan of shared residency. It allows that level of participation, if you reside in the same community. It's unquestionably strange to visit a parent on the weekend and pretty much sit around the house watching TV or playing board games. That's not what the non-divorced families do (except for perhaps an hour or two each week), so it shouldn't really be what the divorced ones do. In fact, the best advice I ever received on how to work with divorced families is to help them "act normal," meaning to do as many things as possible to make the divorce fade into the background and let a normal family life come to the front. That's harder to do when a parent has moved, but it's still possible.

My only divergence with Sam's advice is the idea of developing a second friendship group, which would be pretty tough to create and maintain. Instead, I encourage the distant parent to regularly invite a couple of the child's friends to come along for the visit. That can turn the weekend from a chore to a fun opportunity to spend time in a different city. Some distant parents object to sharing a child with her friends, but by the time a kid is sixteen it's just not normal to spend endless one-on-one time. Parents who've tried this strategy have found it works pretty well and has the advantage of giving them a clearer impression of their child's friends.

Bottom line: The court's standard for child custody is the child's best interest. I agree that your daughter has an obligation to build a good relationship with her dad, but he would be wise to consider her needs and desires and to accommodate them when appropriate. That's what the rest of us do, and while divorce changes many things, it does not change that.

Stepmom's Woes

Dear Dr. Wes and Julia,

My thirteen-year-old stepson has a few issues for which he is getting help. My problem is that his bio-mother doesn't pay attention to him. She only has him come over to her house if we ask, and she never calls to check on him when he is here. I can see that this is hurting his feelings, and despite my suggestion that she call more often, it doesn't happen. How do I help him deal with this consistent rejection? By the way, we live less than two miles from each other, so this is not a problem of physical distance.

Dr. Wes: America is a country of divorce. It's hard to get an exact rate because there are a lot of factors to consider, but what we do know is that most kids today live in something other than the "traditional" or "intact" home. Lots of experts, therapists, politicians, church leaders, and researchers offer advice on how to avoid divorce, but it's unlikely we'll see any reversal of that trend in the near future.

Because remarriage or cohabitation is the norm, there are increasing numbers of stepparents. In some homes, both parents are stepparenting each other's children. In some cases, the divorce is friendly and the stepparents don't have problems with the biological parent in the other home. In other cases, an ugly divorce and custody battle sends the stepparent right into a buzzsaw and, not infrequently, another divorce. And I've just scratched the surface of how complex these situations can become.

You're in a real bind here. The best analogy I can offer you is one I use with foster parents. Regardless of how badly you believe the biological parent is behaving, resist the urge to point that out to your stepson. I'm not suggesting that you overtly deny reality and tell him that his mother is his greatest blessing. Just avoid taking every opportunity to remind him that she's not. Stick to appropriately timed responses like, "I realize how hard this is for you," and then move on. Even if your stepson is saying disrespectful things about his mom, do not get on the bandwagon. Especially avoid getting into any contests or power struggles with his mom, no matter how she may be distancing herself. The best foster parent I ever met worked tirelessly to help the biological mother of her foster children recover from substance abuse. When she failed, the foster parent maintained respect for the biological mother, even while she adopted the children into her home. You've already tried to influence this woman, so you have to move on and quietly help your stepson without threatening the delicate relationship he has with his mom.

Rather than trying to replace her, just reach out as a kind, adult friend. Offer the support you feel the mother is not providing, but let his dad do the parenting and discipline. If your husband is leaving this to you, let him know that this puts you between a rock and a hard place. Too often the primary residential parent in a divorce—be it male or female—starts looking for someone to help raise the children, or worse, take the whole thing over. That's not your job.

Julia Davidson: I'm always surprised when my friends get away with telling their mothers, "I'll be home late, call you later, bye." Mine was always so diligently protective of my whereabouts and wellbeing that, in comparison, I assume other mothers are neglecting their daughters.

Although your stepson is probably hurt by his mother's actions, she may be parenting the best she can and doesn't know any different. It's not a stepparent's place to tell someone else how to parent, but you might consider telling her how you think he feels rather than how you feel. Share with her what he has said to show his disappointment.

So long as you keep the resolution of your stepson's needs as the basis for your conversations, fewer feelings will get hurt. If you're uneasy about talking to her, see whether he would be willing to directly share how he feels and maybe set up a scheduled few days of the month where it's just him and his mom spending time together.

So Much Going on

Dear Dr. Wes and John,

With so many families having to juggle jobs, activities, and schooling, it seems that the home isn't a place where we can actually sit and have an old-fashioned dinner. We try to do this a couple of times a week, but it seems we always have so much going. I'm guessing cutting back in certain areas would be the best thing, but are there any other recommendations?

Dr. Wes: I'm not sure the "old-fashioned family dinner" was ever as common as we think. It sure isn't the standard now. Only 33% of families routinely eat dinner together and half of those do so with the TV on. The real issue is the modern barriers that keep families from spending time together.

Over the years, I've watched many families respond to new technologies that allow us to manage more information, produce more goods and services, and involve ourselves in more *One of the best "tough love" actions my parents ever took was not subscribing to cable or satellite TV.* activities than ever before. Increasingly, this hyper-drive world is too full of possibilities. We've gone from recognizing Type-A personality styles to creating a Type-A culture that lures us into overworking, overspending, over-media consuming, and overactive relaxing. Who has time for dinner? We have drive-thru. Conversation? We have text messaging. Keeping track of what those darn kids are up to? We have cell phones with GPS.

Many wonder why psychopharmaceuticals are now so widely consumed. I believe one under-researched reason is this increasingly manic pace of life, in which people expect too much of themselves and hand down those expectations to their children through the schools, sports teams, jobs, etc. For example, many elementary schools have shortened recess at lunch and dropped it completely in the morning. I vote that we extend recess into middle school to encourage physical activity and leisure time as a way to decompress overstressed kids. Instead, schools themselves are stressed out with arbitrary benchmarks like the inept "No Child Left Behind." No time for silly things like play and recreation. A hyper-drive society creates hyper-drive people, resulting in the kind of family you describe in your comment.

For those wanting to rebel against the machine, try these tips:

- Sit down and make some hard decisions about what is and isn't important to you and decide how to *enact* those priorities over the long haul.

- Pace yourself so that the time spent together doesn't simply reinforce the manic lifestyle. One amped up trip to Disney World isn't as valuable as many short trips to museums, ball games, go-karts, or anything that can be sustained more easily and economically.

- See a financial planner to learn to live on less, leaving less time at work and more time for important things.

- Divide and conquer. Send dad with the young kids and mom with the older ones to do things that fit their age levels, then switch off the next time.

- When two parents are in the picture (divorced or not), it's not sufficient to have one strictly stay-at-home and one peripheral, overburdened, working parent. Both need to be active with their kids, even if that means each works less and involves him or herself more.

- Use your cool smartphone or day planner to schedule time with kids just as you would a meeting with the Executive Vice President of Important Work Stuff. If you take time with kids as seriously as a business meeting, you can beat the hyper-family syndrome.

John Murray: One of the best "tough love" actions my parents ever took was not subscribing to cable or satellite TV. At first, I was jealous of my friends' programming options, but after I spent time watching TV with them, I realized what a waste of time it was. Television has an addictive quality to it, and your brain works slower while watching it than sleeping. If TV dinners have become the norm in your family, give the tube a break for a week. You'll be surprised how little you miss it.

While it is good to share events with the whole family, one-on-one bonding also has its place. Learn about your family members' interests and try participating in their hobbies. If your sister enjoys video games, for instance, try playing some multiplayer games together. If your brother will be acting in a play, make sure to attend a production and congratulate him at the end. You may have to feign interest in subjects you don't care for, but these relationships are investments that will pay dividends the rest of your life.

While it's true that society pressures individuals to work overtime, it also allows plenty of opportunities for wasted time. Media distractions like television and texting can waste hours during the week if you don't make an effort to avoid them. On the other hand, some people try to accomplish too much, and make unwise sacrifices in health and relationships to do so. There will be times of crisis when your urgent needs require every waking hour, but if an ultra-full lifestyle has become your routine, take a moment to reconsider what your real priorities are in life. *The 7 Habits of Highly Effective Teens,* by Sean Covey, contains lots of insight on this topic.

Eating meals together is important, so your family should make every effort to bring everyone together. You may need to be more creative. Try talking to your parents while doing chores or striking up conversation while riding in the car. It is good that you are making an effort to spend time with your family, and it will get easier with practice. Your family provides you with the most important relationships of your life. As they improve, so will your relationships with everyone else.

The Ripple Effect

Dr. Wes: Two days after Father's Day, we buried my father-in-law, Andy Torres. As these things go, it was a good experience; family and friends gathered to celebrate the life of someone to whom they felt genuinely connected. Someone whose brand of fathering had, over the years, deeply affected each father in attendance.

When you're seventy-five, nobody will remember how many nights you were out on the town, or the hours you worked every week.

There exists within each of us who knew him, a part of Andy that will guide our parenting long after he is gone. I know this as a psychologist—that we learn how to treat others by the examples we see in our homes and communities. I know this as a father—that when we offer love and encouragement and hope to our children, they will in turn pass it on. If we are treated with dignity, we will share it.

If we are instead ignored or abandoned or hurt by our fathers, we tend to spread that around too. In my line of work, I see too much of this, usually from men who had children they didn't really intend to have and for whom they didn't get up and do what needs to be done, leaving their sons and daughters to fend for themselves. Research suggests this doesn't turn out very well. Experience confirms it.

For Andy, becoming a father was a promise that he worked to keep until the day he died, one which radiated not only through his biological children and grandchildren, but also through other young people to whom he offered a sort of spiritual parenting. In fact, he fell ill for the last time while preparing to preform his grandson's wedding.

As I left the cemetery, my little boy's hand in mine, it occurred to me that for those of us who make the promise, every day is Father's Day—a time to celebrate the joys and struggles of actively raising our kids. For those who've held back, fearing the commitment or avoiding the responsibility, there is always tomorrow. When you're seventy-five, nobody will remember how many nights you were out on the town, or the hours you worked every week, or how many games you watched on ESPN. They will remember you by the children you raised.

Andy Torres will be fondly remembered.

Ben Markley: We are all directly affected by fatherhood, whether we have a great father, a struggling father, a bad father, or one we never knew. They teach their sons to be men, and their daughters what a real man is.

Good fathers (and mothers!) don't just shape good children. They shape good parents, good spouses, good workers, good friends, good leaders, and good citizens. My grandfather testified to this when he passed away and his family came together to celebrate his life. My father and his siblings carry on the qualities my grandfather exemplified in his life, creating a ripple effect out to each member of his family: humility, hard work, and a quiet joy about life. It was not, however, until the birth of my little nephew Levi last month that I realized the depth of this man's legacy. My grandfather died before Levi was born, but he will still know something of his great grandfather through his mother, his own grandparents, and his uncles and aunts. He will grow up and, hopefully, pass on that part of his great-grandpa to his own children.

I can only hope that one day I will make my own ripples as a father. Until then, I have an excellent father to learn from.

10 PARENT-TEEN CONFLICT

Trust, Respect, and Manipulation

Dr. Wes: Words were once magic in human history. As we evolved the ability to communicate, the richness of our language set the stage for pretty much everything else. Language not only describes our culture, it influences it. Musicians may claim they are just reflecting their (often dysfunctional) world, but they are really defining and influencing ours too. So, if you think of your own words as magical, you'll begin to see which ones do and don't foster helpful thoughts and behaviors in your teen. Several really unhelpful ones on my list include respect, trust, and manipulation. These words create their own stories and rarely are they good ones.

The key to intervening with kids is always to start by unraveling the mystery, not just assigning unhelpful labels that then define how we think and feel about them.

Trust is kind of a silly idea when it comes to teens. In fifteen years of practice I've only met one teenager who claimed teens were trustworthy. Now that she's in college, she admits she was lying. However, *parents* often claim their teens are trustworthy, which never fails to amaze me. In my line of work, I get to hear each week what teenagers do and most of it goes on without parental knowledge. Trust is usually more about parental convenience than a good childrearing strategy.

Respect is formally defined as "having an attitude of admiration and deference; paying attention to and refraining from violating something; or showing consideration or thoughtfulness." That sounds nice, but the average teen brain simply isn't built that way and expecting your kid to be respectful is setting you up for unnecessary disappointment. Back in the days of HBOs *The Sopranos*, Tony took disrespect very personally. He tended to kill you for it.

I'm not too fond of the word "manipulation" either. I call it the M-word and ask families to banish it from their lexicon. It's better to think of the "manipulative teen" as someone trying to get a need met or trying to differentiate herself from her parents without much success. The entire purpose of adolescence is to transition to adulthood, so psychological individuation from parents is not a problem, it's a solution. If parents are too strict, a child will find devious means of achieving this goal. Of course, if parents aren't strict enough, differentiation doesn't create any tension, so there's nothing to push against, which often leads to disaster. Balance is everything.

I always begin by trying to think of how a teen's behavior serves a purpose. I don't always find it, because some behavior is guided by anxiety, depression, or ADHD. But rarely do I find a kid who is just out to jack up the world because it's fun. Yes, they do exist, but if you have one that's really *just* "manipulative," then you're in for a world of hurt that goes beyond what we can address in this column.

As Sam points out below, teens are a constant source of entertainment because they are so mysterious, even to themselves. We've all been there and yet we find the adolescent days puzzling and strange. The key to intervening with kids is always to start by unraveling the mystery, not just assigning unhelpful labels that then define how we think and feel about them, or using wishful thinking about trust and respect to guide our choices.

Samantha Schwartz: For many parents, reading a teen is like trying to read the secret message on a cereal box without a decoder ring, so I'll do my best at decoding. I won't reveal every little lie teens tell their parents, only those that could have a long-term effect on the teen, parent, or both.

Teens often prey on the communication gap between their parents. Whether divorced or just unforthcoming with each other, teens sense any parental discord and use it to their advantage. Your teen could ask you both for money for the same school function and pocket the extra change, or pit you against each other by separately asking each parent to go somewhere, and then letting you fight over the good cop/bad cop roles. By splitting, your teen has found an easy escape to do whatever she wants.

Teens often use a sleepover as a cover for spending time with people you would not like. If a teen attends sleepovers almost every weekend, you have reason to be suspicious. She could easily sneak out to a different friend's house where teens are taking advantage of an out-of-town or inattentive parent. Parents need to discuss their boundaries directly, while always trying to be fair. Although I have no curfew (even when I am with boys), my parents' rule is that I have to text them whenever I change locations and wake them up when I get home. This is pretty fair and allows them to know where I am and that I've come home safely.

It's a major red flag when teens quickly close their laptops or minimize websites on their screens when parents walk in the room. They're likely talking to someone or about something they don't want you to know about. This con is more complicated because they could be hiding anything from a conversation about how to get fake IDs to one about how they snuck out last weekend.

High school attendance offices can't tell the difference between a parent and a kid pretending to be a parent. If a teen's attendance data doesn't match your memory, there's a problem. Your teen could easily call herself in as "absent for a family emergency" and head off to hang out downtown without any adults finding out.

If you think you've been conned, don't jump to conclusions. Try to have an open and honest discussion with your child about your suspicions. If he can prove his innocence, great! If he admits to the con or you have solid evidence, don't heap on the punishments this time. Just let him know you're on to him and that future infractions mean consequences. If your teen isn't admitting to anything and you have no evidence, let him know that you're always there to listen and help if he gets into a tough situation.

Hapless, Unsuspecting Parents?

Dear Dr. Wes and Marissa,

I respect that your experience with teens suggests that "trusting" them often results in their running roughshod over their hapless and unsuspecting parents[14]. However, I remain troubled by this implication of your approach. I don't see how kids who behave principally out of fear of parental punishment eventually become responsible adults, which I define as behaving according to one's ethics and morals. To ask the question bluntly, what's the point of keeping 'em alive through high school if they're just going to kill themselves and others when they leave home and get out from under the parental thumb? When and how do adults learn the difference, for example, between drinking too much at home after work (bad) and drinking and driving (VERY bad), unless they assume increasing amounts of independence and trust as teenagers?

Dr. Wes: I don't see the problem—or our previous answers—quite the way you describe them. Kids aren't tramping over goofy, doormat-like parents. Instead, one of two conditions often exists among "trusting parents." Some believe that "it's those other kids" who go out drinking, drugging and having unprotected sex. They assume their kids are so well-raised and well-mannered that they'd never be drawn to such things. More inexplicable are parents who actually did these untrustworthy things themselves and therefore assume that since they survived adolescence intact, their children will too. They forget that their roles have changed now. They are the parents.

Trust sets parents up for disappointment and their teens for shame. Trusting parents take teen mistakes too personally, which causes them to feel disrespected and betrayed.

Certainly, the road to adulthood is paved with mistakes, mishaps, and foolishness, each of which should be a learning experience. However, that road is a hell of a lot more dangerous now than it was in our teen years. Some sit back as *laissez-faire* or democratic parents and allow

---

14 This column is found in Chapter 4 of this book under the heading "Trust."

teens to find their way with a gentle nudge now and then. Others become controlling autocrats, snoopervising everything our kids do, like the helicopter parents Foster Cline and Jim Fay describe in their book.[15] Trusting parents hope that a child's "inner wisdom" (a commodity yet to be proven in psychological literature) will find solutions while the parent listens empathically. The latter trusts nothing about their child, expecting her to fail at every turn or fall victim to "peer pressure" if allowed outside family influence.

Research instead suggests that an "authoritative" style of parenting is best. Such parents are both demanding and responsive to their kids, setting clear standards for their conduct. They are assertive, but neither intrusive nor restrictive. Their discipline is clear, but supportive rather than punitive. They strive to make teens socially responsible and self-regulating, but realize they will not be capable of sensible autonomy until well past the age of majority.

Authoritative parents do not expect children to accept their judgments, values, and goals without question, and are willing to explain their reasons for taking certain actions. But they do take action. They impart values regarding the treatment of self and others. Yet, nowhere in this literature is the authoritative parent advised to be trusting. He instead recognizes that teens are "born to trouble as the sparks fly upward," while realizing that influence and not control is the best hedge in responding to that reality. Good old "natural and logical consequences" is a valid approach to discipline. Just remember that those consequences include addiction to hard drugs available at our local schools, early pregnancy, and incurable STDs.

But the worst thing about trusting teens is far more basic than all this. Trust sets parents up for disappointment and their teens for shame. Trusting parents take teen mistakes too personally, which causes them to feel disrespected and betrayed. Authoritative parents are able to see teen misbehavior in a developmental context, leaving them free to modify the rules and move on.

Instead of trusting teenagers to do the right thing, set up a method of verification that is age appropriate and diminishes slowly as they work their way out of the home. This holds them accountable while making protection a team effort—not a one up/one down proposition.

---

[15] Parenting with Love and Logic (Cline & Fay, 2006)

Marissa Ballard: I agree with your position to an extent. Overprotective parents handicap their children once they leave the home. But I also believe that parents who give their children too much freedom—and with it a lack of common sense and a realistic comprehension of consequences—similarly hinder the development of their children. My grandmother once told me a story in which she called her mother shortly after she married and yelled at her for never teaching her how to be a housewife. She said that she wished her mother would have made her push a vacuum every now and then, instead of catering to her needs so readily. Parents can instill in their children basic living skills while giving them due freedoms.

As with most things in life, there needs to be a balance, the details of which vary greatly from one family to another. I agree that teenagers should assume increasing amounts of independence, but they also need to be called out when they have made a poor decision. I see the "gradual independence" process Wes suggests much like reeling in a fish. You relax the line a bit, then pull swift and hard when the fish begins to pull in the wrong direction. Teens need that lax line to grow, but it is also essential that they have someone to jerk them back as necessary.

Low-Cut

Dear Dr. Wes and Samantha,

I have a question that's troubled me since my niece was thirteen. She's now sixteen, a well-rounded, active and popular student who has few concerns socially. Her parents care very much about her and seem to use good judgment with her developmental issues, with one exception. I realize fashion trends and peer pressure are strong forces against teen modesty, and my niece has always been eager to wear those popular low-cut tops and camisoles. I'm seeking your opinions on whether young, attractive, and well-endowed girls of this age can "handle" the social situations that such exposure might create. Do parents need to also consider this a potentially risky behavior and provide greater management?

Samantha Schwartz: While I share your concern, you should stay out of this issue or risk alienating both your niece and her mom by offering advice on how she "should" dress. *Maybe* you could play the role of the nice aunt and take her shopping for more appropriate clothes, perhaps as a birthday gift, but be careful.

It's my experience that, while some choose to wear low-cut tops to get undesirable attention, many girls do so simply because they haven't found a style yet that makes them feel attractive without showing some skin. These tops are never really in or out of style—they're just the go-to thing for teen girls who want some attention for how they look, but don't know exactly how to achieve it.

It's the parents' job to draw the line on how low a top can be and to monitor their daughters' clothing choices. Dressing that way sends the wrong message and attracts a caliber of guy that your niece does not want. In fact, I know great guys who would be less attracted to a young woman if she regularly dressed that way.

Parents shouldn't immediately start criticizing a daughter's outfits, however. The mom in your case could have her daughter try on all of her clothes for her, making a pile to keep and a pile to give away. The low-cut shirts have to go. If there's a low-cut top your niece cannot part with, she can try wearing it with a bandeau—a cropped tube top that goes under a shirt.

Next, the mom should help the daughter plan a shopping trip with an older friend or adult whose style she would like to emulate. Your niece's mom should talk to the older friend ahead of time about transitioning out of low-cut tops and into a style that leaves a little more to the imagination.

Dr. Wes: I love Sam's advice, but I'm going to take an entirely different tack. Except for the most blatant exposures of skin, we're long past the point where clothing has much impact on how boys view girls or girls view themselves. It's more like a symptom than a cause. At the risk of being indelicate, the modern teen boy doesn't have to spend more than a couple minutes imagining what's going on beneath a young woman's comely frock. Kids have the Internet, where they can spend endless hours learning all the secrets of human anatomy in excruciating detail. Besides, the real dynamics of teen sexuality don't spring from sexy clothes. They grow out of the age-old process of dating and mating, and that's where you need to put all your energies as an aunt or parent.

I don't see "peer pressure" as the main issue in clothing selection. Sexuality among teens is usually about recreation or competition for dating partners. As young women have gained greater confidence expressing their sexuality, many have leaned away from traditional dating relationships. Girls often feel that sexual availability is the only social currency they have to connect with their male peer group.

That's why our old clichés don't make much sense any more. "A guy who really cares about you" may *not* wait, because in the greater dating pool he doesn't have to. Many "good girls" certainly don't wait because they see no reason to do so, lest they miss out on teen coupling and the perceived benefits that brings. There's no evidence that having early sex is "a sign of poor self-esteem" or "lack of respect for your body," and so on. This trend however, socializes teens in a sexual culture that may not evolve well into adulthood as relationships go from practice to the permanent. So, the clothing choices you note are, at worst, a representation of that trend, but they don't necessarily contribute to or define it.

Bottom line: I wouldn't make my stand on the issue of clothing at all. I'd make it on the larger and ongoing discussion of sexuality—how teens see themselves in the context of relationships, how they enjoy their growth in that area, and how they can protect themselves from the downsides, both emotional and physical. That's a great job for an aunt, as long as you stay square with the parents.

Oppositional Son

Dear Dr. Wes and Julia,

My sixteen-year-old son has been behaving in a progressively worse manner over the past year. He's rude to us, telling us to shut up, get out of his face, and not to tell him what to do. He calls his younger sister names and runs her down. He doesn't come home on time, wants to play computer games straight after school and halfway into the night, doesn't do his school work until the last minute, walks out of the house when we tell him he's grounded, takes our computers apart for upgrades to his, and stays on his cell phone 'til all hours. I recently blocked his phone, but now I have to rely on his friends having their phones turned on when I need to contact him.

I am told by his friends' parents that he is polite and helpful when he is there, but he just doesn't want to have manners at home or help out when we give him chores. We don't have the money for boarding school. Is this normal and should we accept it without a fight, or is there something we can do to change it?

Julia Davidson: Which terms best define "teenager?": (a) sweet and well-mannered; (b) rude and misbehaved; (c) always upset about something; (d) I don't know, he's always gone or sleeping. The correct answer is (e) all of the above. Every teenager is made up of the same basic stuff: Raging hormones, a desire to be an individual, and a heightened sense of whatever they are feeling. However, adding all of the components together can make for an unfortunate result that leaves the teen feeling misunderstood and the parents cut off.

You want to reach out to your son and offer any help and support you can, but he is being ungrateful, rude and apathetic. Now, switch the point of view. Your son is desperate to be an individual, accepted among his friends and on top of his quest for individuality. He has homework and girls, and his parents pressuring him to know what is wrong. From both points of view, someone is in the right and someone is in the wrong. That's the constant gap between parents and teenagers—both sides saying, "I'm right, you're wrong, and *you* need to change."

Let me save you some suspense. Your son isn't going to decide to behave better on his own. Why would he?

As I see it, neither of you is wrong in this situation. You're being the parent: supportive, loving, involved in your teens life; and your teen is being the teenager: moody, surly, and lacking "cool parents." Both of you are doing what is instinctual. However, if neither changes how you react to one another, it will be a long couple of years before anything improves.

I'll offer two golden rules when it comes to teenagers that might help you when it comes to dealing with your son in the future. First, let him come to you. Teenagers are sort of like cats. When they are ignored, they will come to you for attention. I will try and get the most response out of someone who notices me the least. It might take a while, but the less your son feels like he needs to block you out, the more he will open up and feel inclined to share things with you. Second, every teenager needs an outlet. It might be a girlfriend, a sport, sleep, anything healthy that takes the edge off of all the stress. It sounds like your son's outlets are his computer games and cell phone and, by the amount of energy he puts into both, he is probably blowing off a lot of stress.

Although it's unhealthy to have his eyes glued to a screen until the early hours of the morning, perhaps you can reassess this situation and rework his outlet. He likes gutting computers and playing games. Are there any clubs at school or in the community that do that sort of thing? You could also limit rather than eliminate his cell phone use.

It has been said that "raising teenagers is like nailing Jell-O to a tree," but with an extraordinary amount of tolerance and patience on your part, you will come out a happier parent and your son, a more grateful adult.

Dr. Wes: This is a typical family therapy case and I suggest you give that approach some thought. However, I would say it's rapidly moving past normal. You need to remember that you are the parents. Many families are stretched too thin these days, leaving them desperately wishing their kids would "just behave" so they won't have yet another thing to worry about. The nighttime use of cell phones or computers is common and particularly odd to me. Parents are apparently surprised to learn that kids are using their gizmos all night long, so they take them away. Then the kids flip out, screaming, threatening, crying, etc. and, for some reason, the parents give the devices back. Why not suspend the service or shut down the Internet connection until peace resumes? Because many parents find it inconvenient to collect the phones every night or have their kids live out of touch and offline. Same situation with cars. Take them away and parents feel *they've* been grounded, shuttling their teens here and there. So, they give the car back before any lesson is learned, then wonder why their teens don't take them seriously.

Let me save you some suspense. Your son isn't going to decide to behave better on his own. Why would he? As Julia notes, kids are interested in kid things, not adult things. It's our responsibility to make them aware of issues like school, sleep, accountability, ethical behavior, etc., and to hold them to higher standards. Thus, assertive parenting is more crucial in adolescence than at any other time. Kids respect power, not abusive or coercive power, but compassionate power.

Sit down with your son, explain the rules and consequences, and stick to them. He may be a fine fellow, but he does not have a right to

DEAR DR. WES…FOR PARENTS

anything he does not earn himself and use appropriately, nor to come and go as he pleases. This won't make him "respectful," but it will make him consider consequences in deciding whether it's worth it to continue doing what he wants to do. Unfortunately, if things really get out of hand, violence or self-harm may emerge. If it gets that far, do not hesitate to use law enforcement or hospitalization to protect your son and your family. This sounds extreme, but parents must not let their children intimidate them.

Bottom line: If you're not going to dish fair and logical consequences, he's not going to behave. At this point, some of those consequences may need to be extreme in order to get him back in line.

Son Says "No" To Driving

Dear Dr. Wes and Ben,

My son seems very unusual among his peers. He doesn't want to drive. All the other kids got their licenses after driver's ed, but my son isn't interested. I tried to talk to him about why this isn't important to him, but he just says he doesn't see the point. He'll be in college next year and I don't know how he's going to get to a job. Do you have any suggestions?

Ben Markley: My car is currently broken down, and I have very little difficulty getting where I need to go. But I'm still in high school, where you generally have an arsenal of friends and family with cars and licenses who are willing to give you a ride. Your son may not realize that this luxury won't be so readily available in college, especially if his school is far from home.

Granted, if he has an alternate mode of transportation, perhaps this isn't such an immediate issue. Many college students rely on buses and bikes to get around campus, and, by using these services, your son could save a good wad of cash in the midst of high gas prices. This is something that needs to be planned out, however, and not simply assumed.

Yes, senior year is fun, but it's also time to start thinking purposefully about the future. Your son needs to seriously consider his transportation plans. Help him work through these details, since you've probably had to deal with many of them yourself.

Dr. Wes: I agree with Ben. For most teens and adults, owning a car will create more headaches than it cures. With the ever-escalating gasoline prices, your son may be smarter than those of us who've built our lives around the worship of shiny metal boxes. There are many colleges where cars have little use. I just got back from The University of Wisconsin. A whole section of Madison is built around the university, which students use bikes and scooters to navigate. However, it gets pretty cold up there in December, which brings me to the next point.

Unless your son commits himself to life in a city with great public transportation (Chicago, New York, San Francisco, Washington, DC), and he's very smart about how he manages his time, he's going to have a tough time not needing to drive. Likewise, when one chooses any path at age sixteen, to the exclusion of any other, one creates conditions for regret. Sure, your son could learn to drive at twenty-one (or sixty-one for that matter), but he'll lack the crucial period of supervised experiential learning that creates good drivers.

Try to incentivize driving through any means at your disposal, even if he only drives with you in the car for a few years. He doesn't need to go out cruising every evening (at $100 per tankful). He just needs to know how to do it well before he heads off to college. By the way, I've been running into this problem a lot lately. Some kids have an almost phobic reaction to driving. If your son is at that point, I'd drop in on the therapist for some "systematic desensitization" to reduce whatever fears he might have.

Outing A Daughter's Girlfriend

Dear Dr. Wes and Samantha,

I saw your column last fall on same-sex relationships. I've reached a peace about my daughter's sexual orientation, but her girlfriend's family doesn't know. My daughter says I can't tell them because this will cause all kinds of problems for the girl. I am torn about what my responsibility is here. I know how to enforce the rules about sexual contact at home, but doesn't the other parent have a right to know?

Samantha Schwartz: I can see why you want to make sure your daughter is well supervised, but unfortunately, it's really not your place to drag your daughter's girlfriend out of the closet. Coming out to one's

DEAR DR. WES...FOR PARENTS

family is a huge step for anyone, and if this girl is not ready yet, you don't have the right to do it for her. It could cause permanent damage to your relationships with your daughter, your daughter's girlfriend, and also the girlfriend's parents. You may accept your daughter's sexual preference, but not all parents respond well to this kind of news.

Here's what you *can* do. Encourage the girl to come out to her parents. Be a sounding board for both of them. Offer to let the girlfriend rehearse coming out to you. Find out more about her parents so you can gauge how difficult it will be for her. Help strategize the right time and place to talk to her parents about her sexuality. Advise her to come out to a close aunt or family friend first if she thinks she might need an ally. Mediating that discussion yourself would be risky. If her parents are going to react badly to the news, they probably won't want to listen to her girlfriend's parent. Just be supportive, and if the opportunity presents itself, let your daughter's girlfriend know that her parents will love her no matter what and will eventually realize that the personal qualities they love have not changed just because she is a lesbian.

The decision to reveal her sexual orientation is hers alone, and the outcome is far from predictable.

Parents have the right to limit time spent alone in the house with girl- or boyfriends. Her parents won't set those limits because they're still in the dark. Tell your daughter and her girlfriend that until both sets of parents know, you would prefer that they spend most of their time at your house. If you are like most parents and would not let your daughter have sleepovers with a boyfriend, you should make the same rule for her girlfriend.

Finally, I'd like to commend you for accepting your daughter for who she is and trying to meet her needs. I'm sure she appreciates your support.

Dr. Wes: I see teen dating as a team effort, not something inherently conflict-ridden. Unless a dating partner is downright dangerous (and some are), parents should try and welcome their children's romantic interests into the home. This works for two reasons. First, it's simply the right thing to do to maintain influence over your child, which, at this age, is everything. Second, saying "no" is the quickest way to fascinate your kid with someone you despise. "No" is a necessary and powerful word in parenting. Choose wisely when and how you use it. As you've already figured out, this is not one of those times. If the girlfriend is a good person, cares about your daughter, and has her best interests at heart—as much as any teenager can—your support of the relationship is well founded.

However, just as Samantha suggests, teamwork does not explicitly extend to your daughter's girlfriend's family. I realize this is one heck of a dilemma, creating a host of issues you've never even considered before, but stop and think for a moment how much more complicated it is for this girl.

I cannot stress enough how bad an idea it is to rat this girl out to her folks. If she were at imminent risk of harm, using hard drugs, drinking and driving, or having unprotected intercourse, I'd tell you to drop a dime on her. But the decision to reveal her sexual orientation is hers alone, and the outcome is far from predictable. Gay teens are the one demographic that is actually at a higher than average risk of suicide compared to the general population. Many homeless teens are gay, having been thrown out of their family homes for no other reason than their sexual identity. Any estrangement is catastrophic for a youth at this juncture in her life. Even if you knew for a fact that her parents wouldn't go down one of those roads, you are not in a position to accept responsibility for that choice.

I realize certain religious persuasions see homosexuality as constituting imminent risk, but that debate extends beyond the scope of this column. Sam's advice on handling the relationship in your home is wise. The kindness you show your daughter and her girlfriend now will come back to you as she ages and comes to realize how fortunate she is to have parents who took this time in her life seriously and sensitively.

Mom's Boyfriend

Dear Dr. Wes and Samantha,

My mom and dad aren't even divorced yet, but my mom just informed me that she has been dating someone for a while now. I know this is her decision and there's nothing I can do about it, but I just feel like it's too soon and that she should wait until her divorce is final. Worse, she wants me to meet him and spend time with him. This is just too much for me right now. I am already stressed out over everything going on and this only adds to it. I'm afraid if I tell her how I feel and what I think about it, she'll get angry.

Samantha Schwartz: You have a valid reason to be upset. You're still torn up over your parents' divorce and your mom is running to a new guy faster than a shopaholic runs to a designer purse on Black Friday. Worse, she's pushing you into a relationship with a man you don't know, when you are not even used to the idea of life without your mom and dad as a couple.

Though you may not agree with your mom's choices, try to understand her reasoning. She's used to having your dad as part of her basic foundation, and now that relationship has crumbled. Her way to cope may be finding someone to fill the void right away. She may be scared to be alone or looking for a father figure and role model for you.

That said, I agree that she is rushing things and it's definitely too soon for her to be dating. If she were writing us, I would tell her that before she starts going out, she needs to take some time to revaluate her life, her goals, and what she wants in a mate. She should give herself and you time to emotionally process the divorce.

It's fair for you to ask your mom not to date anyone until the divorce is final. I know it's hard to stand up to a parent, but you will feel better about yourself after you do it. Tell her you just need some time. Explain to her that you want her to be happy and find love again, but you are still getting used to the divorce. You can't forbid her from dating him, but if you tell her how uncomfortable it makes you, she may try to accommodate your needs. At the very least, she might better understand your reluctance to spend time with the new man in her life.

When you do talk to your mom, let her know you're willing to meet a new boyfriend once more time has passed, but right now, it's too painful. In a couple months, agree to meet her guy in a low-key setting, like lunch. You don't have to like him right away or spend time alone with him if it makes you uncomfortable, but try to be civil and find common ground to show her you're making an effort.

This must be a difficult time for you, so I hope you've found someone you can talk to and confide in.

Dr. Wes: I wish this sounded odd to me, but from a clinical stand-point it's all too common. I'd suggest you go down to the "Marriage and Divorce" bookshelf and pick up a manual for your mom on how to parent through divorce. Several good ones exist and not one approves of what she's doing. It's not good for you or her. Unfortunately, you've no influence over her dating choices, but you do have the right to protest your involvement, if you do it calmly and sensibly.

People in crises often get a little numb to the world around them. In divorce, we call it "diminished parenting." Your mom expects you to cope with whatever she throws your way, because she feels like she has to cope with whatever is thrown her way. Of course you should be able to depend on her like a rock in the torrent of change you're facing. But just as you need her most, your mom thinks she needs someone else — another man.

For the record, if they go anywhere at all, these rebound relation-ships fail between eighty and ninety percent of the time. So I wouldn't get too worried just yet. However, the fact that she's trying to force you into a premature connection with this guy worries me. Maybe she hasn't read those statistics or taken them seriously, imagining a bright future ahead. Teenagers tend to think they're the exception to the rule where relationships are concerned, and your mom is sort of back in that state of mind right now.

If you can't get her to back off with the new introductions, press for a therapist to get involved. Divorce and custody is a specialized area of practice, so shop around. When you find someone, *sign yourself in as the client,* and then directly ask the therapist to help you explain to your mom why this makes things harder. A good therapist will provide countless reasons why her current tack is unwise and help her under-stand what is and isn't appropriate. She's free to have her romance because she is an adult. She just needs to think twice before forcing anything on you at this vulnerable time in your life.

I could write 90,000 words on this subject and never get to the end of what I've seen. I hope when you're twenty-six, you'll only be able to write about five words in documenting your experience with divorce—*Eventually things turned out okay.*

Tightlipped

Dear Dr. Wes and Kelly,

Our daughter is a high school sophomore this fall. She is very tight-lipped to me, her mother, about anything regarding boys. Do you see this as a problem, or is it to be expected at this age?

Dr. Wes: This depends a lot on how you've developed your conversations about this topic with your daughter over the years, which tends to pay off when it counts. That time for your daughter is now.

Let's assume that you've tried to foster a good working discussion and yet your daughter still seems distant. One obstacle could be an excess of enthusiasm on your part. Perhaps you've done such a good job of pursuing that dialog that your daughter just wishes you'd back off. Some kids imagine their parent trying to relive the joys of adolescence vicariously through them. Another possibility is that your daughter lacks confidence in herself and her dating prospects. So the more you bring up the subject, the more she'll feel like you're pointing out her inadequacies. This is tantamount to having a kid who feels she isn't musically talented being encouraged or even pressured to join every choir in town.

Perhaps your daughter is actually involved with someone and doesn't want to tell you about it. If so, carefully determine why that is. Most kids either openly or secretly want their parents to support their dating life, even as they may tempt our ridicule by their choice of partners. If that's not the case, you probably need to ask her whether you're doing something that offends her or might offend her dating partners. As parents, we're not always good at estimating how our teenagers see us. Perhaps you're saying things she takes as disheartening or she fears you'll unfairly judge her choices.

Give her support and demonstrate your interest in her life, but do so from a greater distance.

Finally, it's possible she leans toward an anxious personality style. If she's a high achiever—or at least very driven in her schoolwork, social life, extracurriculars, career interests, etc.—she may also be a bit more high-strung than her peers. These always seem like the ideal, conscientious kids we'd all like to have. But underneath the super-achiever façade, they're painfully self-conscious and excessively worried (even by teen standards) about what others think and how they will be viewed, particularly by a parent. In that case, focus all your energies on being supportive and encouraging and very little on pushing and demanding, which always backfire with the anxious kids.

Kelly Kelin: Throughout this awkward transition from childhood to adulthood, you may notice your daughter's demeanor drastically change. And as much as you want to help her through these trying times, in the end you may find it better to show support, while allowing her to flourish on her own terms. She will soon be embarking on the confusing journey we call adulthood. Not only is she changing physically, but emotionally and mentally as well. She'll begin experiencing new things, some of which you will know nothing about.

Your daughter's secrecy regarding boys is completely normal, especially for teenage girls. Yes, there are some who have no problem disclosing information to their parents regarding their love life. However, most girls tend to be more modest. Take a look at this situation from her perspective. When you were her age, were you outspoken to your parents about boyfriends? Another possibility is that your daughter may simply not be as boy crazy as many of the girls her age are. Maybe she just hasn't found the right guy to introduce you to.

It's only natural for you to be concerned, but your daughter is only a sophomore. If you want her to open up, give her time and space. As much as you want to be involved in her life, the more you push the more she may continue to shut you out. Instead, give her support and demonstrate your interest in her life, but do so from a greater distance. Let her know that if any problems or questions do come about, you will be there with the answers.

Her tight lips will only become a problem if you notice it affecting her negatively. If she becomes completely aloof about her life, then you should have greater concern. Until then, continue to ride this rollercoaster. In the end, she will appreciate it.

Favoring An "Easy" Child

Dear Dr. Wes and Samantha,

I'd like to be closer to my teen daughter (age thirteen) who is suddenly pulling away in favor of friends. I realize this is part of the natural independence process, but here is my dilemma. We have two children, the daughter and a ten-year-old son. He is happy, friendly, emotionally attentive and considerate. He is outgoing and pleasant and enjoys time with Mom. He physically resembles his dad, but his personality is similar to mine, so it's an easy relationship. My daughter is more independent and willful, physically resembling me but different personality-wise. She is shy by nature, but is suddenly a bit more irritable towards us. I am concerned about treating them equally. I love them both, but he is easier to be around and I worry about favoring him. How do I reconcile these feelings?

Samantha Schwartz: I want to commend you for being so in touch with your feelings about your children. Not all parents realize when they're choosing favorites, and it sounds like you know you should resist the temptation to do so as much as possible.

It's totally natural to feel closer to one of your children when the other is going through a difficult phase. The key word here is *phase.* Your teen daughter is not going to ignore you to spend time with her friends forever, and unfortunately, your son won't stay a mom-adoring, ten-year-old delight, either. Right now, he is the one with whom you connect because he wants to be around you, which makes you feel needed. Your daughter, on the other hand, is experimenting with independence and that's okay.

Remember, you don't have to like your daughter through every minute of this phase; you just have to love her. And it's not that you love your son more right now, but rather that you just like him better because your personalities match. She may drive you crazy, but she'll always be your daughter. It's also important to pick your battles right now. A little more eyeliner than you approve of? Let it go. Gobs of eyeliner, a mini-skirt and fishnet tights? Take a stand.

During this phase, fights will abound, so you'll want some positive interactions to balance the negative ones. Find something you like to do together, even if it requires some compromise on your end. Bear with her through a dumb reality TV show, offer to straighten her hair, or laugh with her at YouTube videos. Show her you want to spend time with her whenever she's interested.

Despite natural disagreements during this phase of her life, I predict that you'll end up good friends. Sometimes having opposite personalities makes for a great relationship in the long run. If your daughter is similar to your husband and you like him, you'll eventually like her.

Dr. Wes: Every week it gets harder and harder to match Samantha's advice. Thankfully, she only has a couple of weeks left to show me up, then off to college where she belongs. I agree with everything she suggests and I'd only add the following philosophical tip. Parenting is by far the most selfless act we do as modern Americans. In previous generations, this was not so. We raised kids for labor on the farm, to take care of us in our old age, and to provide grandchildren to do more of the same. Today, the act of raising a child has mostly spiritual and emotional benefits, which is why I'm such an advocate of planned pregnancy. Each of us needs to prepare as much as possible before taking on this important role. Our little way to change the world.

> *The best thing you can do over the next few years is to transcend your ego.*

Unfortunately, the higher ideals of parenting fade into the fog of adolescence as kids reach the age of thirteen, regardless of how well childhood started out. So, this may not get any better until your daughter is out of the home. That's actually one of the reasons I love working with this age group and writing about them—because they are so interesting, complex, and unpredictable—and in the end, the rewards are tremendous.

The best thing you can do over the next few years is to transcend your ego. Think first about your daughter's real needs (and I don't mean an iPod Touch). Try not to take her distancing personally. Demand that both your children be ethical and moral people, and hold them to reasonable standards, no matter how they may resist or hate you for it. Accept graciously that they will rarely be appreciative or respectful until their mid-twenties. Around then, if you do your job correctly, your daughter will awaken one day and gasp, "Oh, my God, Mom was so right about [fill in the blank]." And that is as it should be.

Be patient. The pathway from child to adult lies unavoidably along the stressful years of adolescence. It is up to you to manage how that relationship works, even if your daughter holds all the power to engage in it.

Spying

Dear Dr. Wes and Marissa,

We've been worried about our teenager. I won't give the details, but she's done some things that concern us. We've been reading her diary and things are really pretty bad. Now, we have to figure out how to respond, but the way we got our information makes that difficult. How should we proceed?

Marissa Ballard: I regret to inform you that you have just killed any chance of this situation going well. It's never easy to approach your child about behavior you disapprove of, but the fact that you went behind her back and violated her privacy puts you in a very bad position.

By reading her diary you have ruined her trust in you. Children need to know that their home can be a place of solitude and safe haven. Now that you've breeched that, whatever good intentions you had will be overshadowed by your actions. Of course you want to help your child, but this should not have been your way to find out what is going on in her life.

There's only one thing that you can really do at this point. Sit her down and explain how you found out the information, then tell her how you feel about what's going on in her life. By saying you're sorry for going through her things, your chances of reaching through to her increase.

I wish you had told us what you found in her diary because "really pretty bad" can be interpreted in many different ways. Also, I'm very curious to know whether she's done anything in the past to indicate she might be hiding things from you. What made you want to read through her diary in the first place? Though it might make you cringe, there are many things in your daughter's life that you'll never know about. Whether that is a good or bad thing is hard to determine.

I hope that in the end, you will realize that spying on your daughter is not something you should ever do again unless it is absolutely necessary. Your daughter will eventually have to get over the fact that you read her diary, but I'm sure it will take some time.

Dr. Wes: It's called Double Take because Marissa and I don't completely agree on some topics. Before I dissent, however, let me agree that spying on kids' private writings is *usually* a big mistake. However, there are a very few times when it may be justified.

The goal of adolescence is to get out alive, childless, educated, disease-free, and without an addiction or serious criminal record. Thus, before spying on your child, you have to decide whether the information you gather is likely to be: (a) concerning enough to justify an otherwise unethical behavior on your part; and (b) worth risking your relationship with your teenager, as Marissa has aptly portrayed. Ponder why it has become necessary to take such measures. If you haven't set a foundation for dialog already, you may have missed your chance for an easier solution.

For example, if you learned that your daughter has a serious drug addiction, then a part of the treatment plan is for privacy to go out the window. That's a topic for another column, but for now consider "serious addiction" to include habitual use of cocaine, methamphetamine, LSD, inhalants, crack, etc. Whether marijuana and alcohol use justifies this level of spying depends on the use pattern and level of impairment you see in your teen. In any situation where addiction is concerned, however, I'd opt for random UAs before I'd ever read a diary.

Regarding sex, if you believe your teen is living on the edge, having poorly protected sex with multiple partners, or exposing herself to disease, you're obligated to get to the bottom of the matter. Here, the only useful test is for pregnancy or STDs and that is closing the barn door after the cows have stampeded out. If you *do* have probable cause to fear these things, spying may become necessary, but only after you've exhausted the more ethical options we propose in other columns. If serious crime, violence, suicidal ideation, or a "hate list" of kids your teen would like to knock off (I wish I were exaggerating) is involved, you are justified in employing more aggressive surveillance tactics in order to save your child. Short of these scenarios, spying wreaks more havoc than help.

It's always better to sit down and talk about these issues, get the truth on the table, and seek help as a family. Spying should be the very last thing parents try, and they should feel guilty at every turn in doing it. Unfortunately, at this level of severity, some kids have long-since shut out their parents, bringing us to the final problem with espionage.

There's a story from World War II that is apparently a myth, but illustrates your dilemma. In 1940, Winston Churchill supposedly learned in advance of a German plan to bomb Coventry, England, yet he did nothing to prepare its citizens. To have done so would have revealed that the Allies had broken the Enigma code, allowing the Germans to reconfigure their equipment and causing even more harm in the long run. You are in a similar position. If you reveal what you've learned, as Marissa suggests, and confront your daughter, you'll create a breach in the relationship from which you may never recover. Your influence will be shot to hell just when you need it most.

In order to resolve this dilemma I would offer the same advice I would have given Churchill: Be sure that the end justifies the means. If your daughter is in imminent danger, then reveal your secret and get her help. She'll hate you now and love you much later. If the problems aren't really as severe as you suggest, then perhaps you shouldn't act on this information, should cease gathering any more of it, and instead find a more honorable way to bring this concern to your daughter's attention.

Too Much Work?

Dear Dr. Wes and Samantha,

How many hours are too many for a teenager to work? My son really has a good work ethic and a pretty good job for being sixteen. But I think he works too much and that he's sacrificing his teen years. He doesn't have to earn that much money. We're blessed with two incomes. What is a good way to know how much is too much?

Dr. Wes: I know a few people who'd like to trade their kid in for yours. A young person with a good work ethic isn't rare, just not as common as we might like. Sam makes some good points below and I'll add three, more subtle issues, that a hardworking teen may face.

Over the last thirty years, kids have been earning more money. Since most have their necessary expenses paid and very few save, they end up with a lot of discretionary income early in life. They can afford cars, computers, game systems, and all the other accouterments. Any wonder they're a major marketing demographic? But when teens go off to college or into the workforce, boom: all those bucks go into making ends meet. Young adults who've worked since they were thirteen find their standard of living has collapsed.

The second problem is whether all that work really pays off in the long run. The goal of adolescence isn't to see who reaches age twenty with the most prizes. It's to prepare for adulthood. Recent research indicates that kids who work more as teens tend to make better salaries as adults, which seems counterintuitive if you put your hopes and dreams on getting a good education. Who would have thought working five years behind the McDonald's counter predicts future income? But what's probably going on is a lot like

Teach him this balanced lifestyle while he's young because many adults still struggle with this issue.

what you see in your son. A teen who works his butt off will work just as hard as an adult. Some of that is experience and some just talent and genetics. On the other hand, it's easy for kids to devalue school when they're making good bank at a part-time job and the costs and consequences of prioritizing their values in that way only show up later.

Finally, I am worried about the level of stress we're putting on our kids in school, at home, and in the workplace. If you feel your son is overtaxed, advise him to cut back. This is really tricky to detect. Kids are pretty resilient and they often won't show signs of stress until things get pretty rocky. Help your son find and keep balance in his life, and things will go better for him in the all-important long run.

Samantha Schwartz: I don't think there's a "right" number of hours a teen should be working. Since money-making is not essential for your family, it depends on what your and your son's priorities are. While it's possible that he just loves to work, he could also be doing it because he's not enjoying other parts of his life and needs a way to fill his time.

Talk with him about why he works so much. Ask what he likes about work and about the friends he's made there. Also, find out whether he's saving for something particular or if he's looking to get promoted at work. Listen to his explanation, but also consider the following factors:

Is he feeling challenged in school? If he's making good grades while working a ton of hours, his course load may be too easy. While it's a little late in the year to change his schedule, keep this in mind next fall. In the meantime, look for classes offered elsewhere in your community or at a community college. Suggest he pick something he's interested in. On the other hand, if he isn't making good grades, he needs to work less and focus on his schoolwork.

Is he involved in any group activities? If not, suggest he cut back hours to become part of the exciting opportunities that high school has to offer. Sports, music groups, and clubs are all great places to meet people and they're usually open to new members year round. If he meets new people with similar interests, he may spend more time with them and less at work.

Remember that he cares a lot about his work, so he may not welcome these suggestions at first. Explain that he'll be working for the next fifty years of his life, but he'll only be in high school once, and you want him to enjoy it. As Wes points out, it's best to teach him this balanced lifestyle while he's young because many adults still struggle with this issue. Pushing him out of his comfort zone may be difficult at first, but he'll eventually appreciate your help.

Parents Made Mistakes as Teens

Dear Dr. Wes and Samantha,

My husband and I have a new baby and are discussing certain parenting dos and don'ts. One thing that keeps coming up is what we should tell our kid about our pasts. For example, should we admit to him that we tried marijuana? Is it hypocritical to tell him not to do things we did? I say I'll flat lie to him about it, but my husband disagrees.

Samantha Schwartz: I can see both sides of the argument. On one hand, you don't want to say, "don't smoke pot" and feel like a total hypocrite. On the other, you don't want your son to make your use of pot an excuse for him using it. Talking to your kids about your past is like baking a soufflé: it's all about the timing.

Set the standards for your kids early and explain your mistakes later. Discuss these issues consistently, not just once they reach key ages. They'll find out information about drugs and alcohol anyway, so it's better for them to hear it from you. Here's a basic outline of ages when they might be ready to discuss these things:

Age 5. Explain why alcohol is something only Mommy and Daddy can drink. Tell them about the law and how it protects kids' minds while they're still developing by outlawing alcohol for minors. Also explain that they are not allowed to take medicine without asking you because it could hurt them.

Age 8. Bring up smoking. Explain what cigarettes can do to their bodies and the concept of addiction.

Age 10. Discuss more serious drugs.

Age 12 and up. Ask about what other kids are doing and if they've been offered anything. Tell them you disapprove of alcohol and drug abuse, but if they have any questions, you're happy to answer them, and if they get into trouble, they should feel free to call you for help. Let them know that there will be consequences, but that you care more about their safety than punishing them.

All ages. Teach them how to say no; that other parents may not have taught their children the same lessons and that it's their jobs to know better.

If they don't ask a specific question about your personal history, don't tell them anything. They probably aren't ready to hear it. When they are, they'll prod you like toothpicks into a soufflé to find out. Then you can divulge information that is appropriate for their age. If you haven't stressed the repercussions of something yet, don't tell your kids you did it. Later you can

Your history is exactly that, a story you tell (or don't tell) about the way things were for you.

say, "I made a big mistake." They'll probably disapprove of your actions, which is exactly how you want them to react. They may ask why you didn't tell them the full story when they were younger. Just explain that it was an issue of maturity and you wanted to make sure they were ready to hear and understand it.

Dr. Wes: We always stress that you should act the way you want your kids to act; behave in the way you want them to behave. If you don't, they will interpret your directives as nothing but a bunch of empty platitudes.

Luckily, your history is exactly that, a story you tell (or don't tell) about the way things were for you. Your past mistakes are far less important in how your child will develop solid character and values than how you conduct yourself in the present. If you still like to hit the bong now and then, or close down the bar on a Friday, don't expect your son to see any problem with doing that himself. It won't matter how often you point out that he's a child and you're an adult.

If instead you see your drug use as an indiscretion of youth, and one you regret, you may at some point want to share the worst aspects of substance abuse with your child. If you think it was super-fun, I'd leave that out of the discussion for many years to come. Better to say, "When I was a child, I thought as a child. Now I'm the parent and my job is to send you down the best path I can."

You've actually hit on one of the most overrated problems of parenting by the way: fear of hypocrisy. Too many parents think back to their own adolescence and realize all the dumb things they did. Then, they either panic and try to lock their kids in their rooms until they're twenty-one, or give up and say, "Oh well. I lived through it. He can too," and let their kids do as they wish. This leaves teens who rebel against unreasonable authority versus those whose parents are too intimidated to step up and remember a simple fact. They aren't teenagers anymore.

Being a parent means doing parent things, just as being a kid means doing kid things. Kids get in trouble and parents dish out the consequences. In this biz, we call it hierarchy. As long as you remain in charge and offer a solid authoritative parenting style based on a good relationship, you'll be fine.

John Mellencamp, that great philosopher, offered some good advice when he said, *"Seventeen has turned thirty-five, I'm surprised that we're still livin'. If we've done any wrong, I'm hopin' that we're forgiven."*[16] Don't drag your youthful mistakes into the present. Just focus on how smart you are now and how much you can help your son be smart too.

Someday your son will need forgiveness, but for now he just needs you to get him pointed in the right direction.

---

[16] From the song *Cherry Bomb,* on the album Lonesome Jubilee, ©2005 John Mellencamp.

Young Adults Living At Home

Dear Dr. Wes and Miranda,

Can you give our family tips on dealing with young college students still living at home? We don't seem to be off to a very good start this fall on how to manage rules and responsibilities.

Dr. Wes: We're seeing the trend you're describing right now due to the ongoing economic downturn. Not only are more late teens staying at home after high school to cut expenses, but many college grads are moving back for the same reason. Because American society shifted away from this model in the 1940s and 50s, we have little leftover experience to draw on.

The desired lifestyle of modern young adults runs about ninety degrees perpendicular to that of their parents, which creates unending potential for daily conflict. It's hard enough for young adults to manage boundaries and responsibilities with roommates or live-in dating partners. It's even more challenging when your roommate is your mom and you're fresh out of adolescence with its many parent-child conflicts.

My best advice for families at this juncture is to make a kind but explicit policy that, after high school graduation, living at home becomes a privilege. While we generally agree on what is acceptable for teens, there's little consensus about young adults, which means each family gets to set up a reasonable roommate agreement based on their own unique situation. To do this, everyone needs to sit down and agree on a contract, and parents must follow-through with eviction if the conditions aren't met. Young adults should hold a job or have student aid to cover a small part of their expenses. For those not in school, the work expectation and financial contribution should be higher. Parents should also consider charging a small rent based on their child's income, and then if possible, save those funds to help him or her attain an apartment later on.

Miranda Davis: As the economic downturn continues, fewer students are choosing to pack up their belongings and head off to different parts of the country for college. More are living at home to attend nearby universities. This isn't a bad option, considering tuition is rising and prospects of getting a job have dimmed. It's become less important to pay for "the college experience" and more important to leave school with a good education. However, living at home presents its own challenges.

While Mom's home-cooked meals and a life without crazy room-mates may seem appealing, living at home can restrict college social life. When setting the boundaries, parents need to remember that once children hit eighteen they become young adults and many rules must be relaxed if they have any chance of working.

On the flip side, students need to remember that their childhood home doesn't suddenly transform into a dorm. He or she may be able to stay up all night blaring music and go to a class at noon, but parents will still have to get up at 7:00 a.m. for work. Being considerate will make the transition from dependent child to semi-independent young adult go more smoothly. In addition to Wes's list, here are some key issues to get the conversation started:

- **Laundry:** Who will take care of the student's dirty laundry?
- **Meals:** Will the student eat with the family? Who will cook when it is "after hours," or when parents aren't cooking a meal?
- **Curfew:** Will you have one? Will there be an expectation of quiet hours?
- **Special Visitors:** This is a big one. What kind of visitors, especially potential dating partners, will be allowed, and can they stay the night?

If you start the conversation early, these pitfalls can be avoided and an equally wonderful college experience can be had.

The Kids are Alright

Dr. Wes: This is our last Double Take of the year. In 2007, John, Julia, and I discussed teen sexuality, sex offending, our increasingly manic lifestyle and the effect it has on teen mood, sleep, and the ability to focus in school. We prompted online debates on all sides of the issues, some of which were exceptionally intelligent. We've debated the wisdom of public policy as it pertains to teen sexuality, even provoking a response from the former Attorney General. We've offered guidance for kids struggling with school, love, their parents, their emotions, and their peers. We've addressed suicide, diagnosis, therapy, bullying, shyness, anger, teen technology, diet, leaving home, eating disorders, violence, and college prep. Just this week, the news reassures us that the pregnancy of sixteen-year-old Jamie Lynn Spears will "promote a national dialog on teen pregnancy." How nice for the nation to join us here at Double Take. We've been discussing it for about three years now.

Every generation is sure that its teens are the worst behaved in history, which then becomes expressed through its media, conversation, attitudes and behaviors. As but one example, America has become far too interested in trying teens in court as adults, believing somehow that imprisonment with violent adult offenders will set those pesky kids back on the right road.

There follows an inevitable "Kids are Alright" backlash chastising the teen-bashers and reminding us that the vast majority of young people become reasonably competent adults. Only a fraction fall among the throes of the addicted, the criminal, the failures at life. In the end, teens are like everyone else, a complex mix of good and bad, right and wrong, astonishing cruelty and unanticipated humanity. A love 'em, fear 'em, or hate 'em approach is foolishly reductive.

Make a special effort to remember what's good about your children and share it with them often. Ask for nothing in return and expect very little.

The holiday season is however, a fine time to emphasize what we really like about our teens. I always try and remember my children's unexpected acts of kindness—those moments of insight and growth, occasions of exuberant discovery or poignant words—all of which makes me remember why I desperately wanted to have them in the first place and still do.

I spend most of my life—thirty hours out of a fifty-hour work-week—standing by kids and/or their parents as they face each other in moments of pain and desperation, terrified that their struggle has reached a turning point from which they will never recover. Will these kids become the adults who reflect back on their adolescence and their home life with resentment and disappointment, mirroring that of their parents? Or will they exit this stage of life emotionally whole and psychologically intact? During those moments, I like to tell the parents stories of my happy times with my children and ask them to think of their own, to recall why they desperately wanted their kids.

This holiday season, make a special effort to remember what's good about your children and share it with them often. Ask for nothing in return and expect very little. I remember the times my dad did this for me, yet he died having no idea how valuable those comments were, because I hadn't yet fully realized it myself. Teens are not thankful for these little things until they pass our shadows as adults.

Your offerings of appreciation will impact their lives long after the Wii, Xbox, and PlayStation are obsolete.

Julia Davidson: This time of year, it seems obligatory for children to set aside differences with their parents in order to receive their gifts, and for parents to force a cheerful family atmosphere to conform to holiday sentiments. Regardless of how many slammed doors, rolled eyes, and You're-Not-the-Boss-of-Me-type comments kids have let fly this year, the holidays offer a good opportunity to reflect on how we've all changed, and to get a fresh start and strengthen family ties. There's no instant holiday fix for poor teen-parent relationships, but being able to look back and appreciate each other can put things in perspective.

Remember to always look at the big picture and not all of the little bits and pieces that made it up. There's always going to be strife between parents and teens. Families wouldn't solve any problems if there wasn't. Looking back at our parents and seeing that, yes, they may have taken away our cell phones and yelled at us a few times, but they still had our backs every time something went wrong. None of our seemingly life-altering fights lasted more than a few minutes. Be proud that both teens and parents remained somewhat civil with one another during a time of raging hormones for us, and midlife crises for you.

Another way to look at parents is to put aside all of the parental duties that bug us, and see them as having friendly intent, always supporting us—be it through sports, the arts, or financially. They're great for conversation and games, and no matter how mad we make them, they find a way to love us. Even though it may seem like a constant uphill battle, parents are eager for us to succeed, and to be happy and safe. Many seem overly strict or protective, but it's a crushing blow to lose a child or to see them unhappy. Parents do almost anything to avoid either one.

We are the jewels of our parents' eyes. Appreciating what they do, even if we can't stand them while they're doing it, will make our relationship stronger this holiday season and beyond.

11 LIVING IN THE REAL WORLD

Explaining the Inexplicable

Dr. Wes: In many ways, it is harder to help our children put the Virginia Tech tragedy[17] into a sane context than it was the events of September 11, 2001. Those horrors happened in big cities to people whose lives seemed different from ours, farther from our reality. The killers were foreign nationals who saw themselves in a vast political struggle that few of us really understood. The VT shooting happened in a small state college town. The victims were kids like those we send off to college every fall and receive back for Christmas, summer break, and occasional laundry duty. The shooter was their dorm-mate, albeit a strange and menacing one. VT is more reminiscent of Columbine or the recent Lancaster County (Pennsylvania) incident. Our neighbors killing our neighbors. Kids killing kids.

How do we explain this to children who increasingly see the world as a frightening, dangerous, and bizarre place into which they should not venture too far? How do we use something senseless to teach them

---

[17] This column was written in April 2007, after a mentally ill gunman shot and killed thirty-two people and wounded twenty-five others at Virginia Tech, before committing suicide. Many in our University town felt a special connection to the community of Blacksburg, Virginia and its immense sense of loss. The next day, as we were about to send this column to press, someone called in a bomb threat to Lawrence public schools, panicking parents and forcing a lockdown of the attendance centers.

something valuable? How do we allay unnecessary fears while encouraging personal safety awareness?

The struggle became even more immediate when, as I was writing this column, another disturbed person called in a threat to our own community, leading schools to lockdown and causing parents great anxiety. Today, we offer our thoughts on how to put all of these incidents into perspective.

Restore faith in order. While watching the towers burn on the morning of 9/11, my then four-and-half-year-old daughter asked, "Isn't that where we were going to go?" I confessed that the World Trade Center was on our travel itinerary that year. "Hm," she said thoughtfully. "Maybe they can put the towers back up." Against a backdrop of chaos, she reminded me of the importance of normalcy in children's lives. She needed to be reassured that order would be restored, even if those two buildings would never rise again.

There is no lesson more critical for today's teens than one that encourages them to treat each other with dignity and love.

Such is the case with Virginia Tech. Our kids need to know that despite the disorder, the world is still turning. The adults have things under control. In the days ahead, the very best thing each of us can do as parents is to try and remain calm. Even as threats continue or other incidents happen, we must above all else keep our heads. To do otherwise is to invite more of the same, which is the very purpose of terrorism: to cause fear that exceeds any realistic threat, leaving us off-kilter, anxious, willing to act out against each other and add to the emerging mayhem.

Control generalization. On Monday, in Virginia, one man killed thirty-two people. Billons more did not. A tiny fraction of humanity is capable of these acts. A few others take advantage of the fear they create. Many of these folks are mentally ill, but the preponderant majority of those with mental illnesses would never harm anyone and are themselves unfairly stigmatized, ignored, or maligned. There are far more acts of kindness per minute in our world than displays of brutal violence. Were this not true, our news would be filled with shocking accounts of good people doing kind things, and we would take for granted the commonality of evil.

Discourage obsessing on "why." In our search for order, we easily slide into the illusion that if we could just explain why someone would do such a thing, then we could find peace and move on. Cooler heads remind us that attempting to make sense of senseless things, or seeking meaning in psychopathic acts only undercuts our own mental health. Instead, we must help our kids understand that the real order of things comes from our families, communities, schools, and support systems. It will never come from the analysis of a deeply disturbed young man or pondering his motives for mass murder.

Focus on love and healing. The most heroic act I've ever seen was the response of the Amish community to the murder of their little girls in a country school. Even in mourning, they reached out to the family of the shooter, offering forgiveness and inclusion to his wife and children. As we examine the VT incident, it is easy to be reviled, angry, hateful. But we need to teach our children that real character comes from how we love each other and how we put that love into action.

Apparently, the shooter, Cho Seumg-Hui, was yet another bullied teen. While this does not excuse his own violence, the lesson of the Amish practiced by each of us every day might lead someone away from such acts. There is no lesson more critical for today's teens than one that encourages them to treat each other with dignity and love. Not just because a small act of kindness early in life may stem the tide of a deteriorating personality, but because it is the right thing to do.

John Murray: We should be mindful of this tragedy, but there is a point at which rubbernecking gives way to irreverence. Our media squeezes every drop of attention it can from disaster, and this case is no exception. Particular blame goes to NBC for reporting on the photo/video collage Cho mailed to its office. This gives would-be killers assurance that their ravings will be published should they choose to follow Cho's example.

The shooting episode has also been marked by too much hindsight. Would stricter gun-control laws have averted this tragedy? As a previous mental patient, Cho was already barred from purchasing a firearm. So, when asked about his medical history, Cho simply lied. If a psychopath is willing to break the law, it's unlikely more gun control will change their actions. Should Cho have been submitted to more vigorous psychological testing? They tried that too, but options are limited when a patient resists therapy.

Heroes surface during every tragedy. One particularly touching example was VT Professor Liviu Librescu, who barricaded the classroom doors with his own body. While his students were able to escape through the window, Librescu was shot in the act of heroism. There were at least four other resistance attempts, all from persons who appeared to live ordinary lives. My uncle was an ordinary worker at the World Trade Center. But when crisis struck, he rushed into the falling towers to help rescue people stuck in the broken elevators. He did this first during the attack in 1994 and then again in 2001, at which time he died.

Are there people around us who would give up their lives for a stranger? Yes, but for the most part we don't know who they are until the moment comes.

Finally, as Wes points out, we must all forge relationships with the disparaged. While it's no excuse to go on a rampage, Cho's loneliness probably played a factor in his decision to murder. I didn't have many friends when I was younger and I will always remember the few kind people who cheered me up. The next time you encounter a "loner," try and strike up a conversation.

Economic Worries

Dr. Wes: In spring 2008, Double Take warned families that the United States economy was headed into the tank, and suggested ways to prepare a generation of young people raised when big credit bought lots of cool stuff. Freshly returned from Washington, DC—the seat of dysfunctional government[18]—I can firmly say in as calm a voice as possible, "Things aren't looking up."

I don't care who you blame, but polls show that Americans no longer imagine a better world for their kids than the one we grew up in. So, in an effort to help prepare for that difficult reality, Double Take will continue discussing how to help teens cope, manage money and anxiety, and develop workable post-high-school plans.

---

[18] This column was written in August 2011, a week after Congress deadlocked on a debt reduction scheme, nearly shutting down the government and forcing the United States into default. At the last minute, an imperfect compromise was reached. I happened to be attending a conference in Washington, DC at the time.

Here's lesson one: Don't freak out. I realize this is difficult. I had my teenager with me in Washington, DC and I'm pretty sure I did some muttering about the fall of western civilization, before launching into a series of apologies to statues of Thomas Jefferson.

Teens certainly won't learn anxiety management watching our leaders. Today, politicians seize on political events to *raise* public anxiety while pointing angry fingers. If your kid treated others this way, I hope you'd ground her and sell her car, Xbox, and iPod on eBay. When teens see that kind of behavior modeled by nationally televised adults, they lose all respect for our institutions and hope for what they can offer us. In such times, they need to have twice as much faith in you as a parent and the hope you offer them, even as you may be fearful yourself.

I spent plenty of time at the Franklin Delano Roosevelt Memorial last week, contemplating and apologizing. It offers a sober reminder that we have been here before as a nation, and still, we found a way. Double Take will do our small part to help you and your teens find yours.

Miranda Davis: I could not agree more. Anyone with an Internet connection or a TV can tell that government "of the people, by the people, and for the people" has become increasingly disconnected from the people. Teens care about these issues, but just as Wes says, they ignore politics because of the immature antics of the politicians.

Finances are a big part of growing up in today's world. Life during and after college is becoming this dark, scary blur for us. As teens, we are not versed in every detail of debt talks and congressional sessions, but we are fully aware of the seemingly endless economic downturn. The recession has affected our daily lives in countless ways. At school, teachers hesitate to print worksheets because the district doesn't have enough money for paper. At home, parents tell us to reduce our spending, or get a job. Some have lost theirs. And so we teenagers are lost right now. We're told to have fun and enjoy our youth, while, at the same time, asked to take on the responsibility of the real world.

If you are a teen and you're not scared of what will come within the next several years, you aren't paying attention. The world we live in has changed. We can no longer be materialistic creatures and we're learning the hard way that we have to manage our money wisely. As a high school senior, most of my nightmares consist of how to pay for college and what to do after I get my degree. The recession has changed this part of my life the most. A college degree is no longer a ticket to a good job. The fear of supporting ourselves, with jobs so scarce, is a reality we will all eventually face. These are the times when nice cars or closets filled with new clothes become irrelevant, and a good work ethic, initiative, and determination are our best hope to succeed.

Holocaust Museum

Dr. Wes: My twelve-year-old daughter and I were visiting the Holocaust museum exactly two weeks ago to the hour of the recent shooting there.[19] It's the busy season in DC as spring yields to an oppressively hot and humid summer. When we arrived at the museum around 8:45 a.m., a line had already formed for same-day passes. My daughter held our place while I got us bagels at the museum's café across the alley. It's the only café I've visited with an x-ray and metal detector at the door.

Pandora was given a sealed box full of all the evils of mankind. Her unfortunate curiosity led her to open the box, unleashing its sinful power. Yet, within the box remained one thing: Hope.

Our early Metro ride paid off. We got a 10:15 a.m. entry. I made my second run of the day through the metal detector, this time at the museum entrance. My daughter impatiently wondered why they needed so much security. "Who would hurt a museum?" she complained. "That's just stupid." I reminded her that this was not her first visit here and she might consider what this museum stood for—a tribute and remembrance to six million people who were murdered by a sovereign state just eighteen years before I was born. In that context, it would not seem shocking for someone to do something crazy to this particular museum.

Entering that morning, guard Stephen Johns ushered us out of the way so the 10:00 a.m. group could line up and the incoming crowd could file through security. He was firm but polite. No nonsense. Very professional. I only know his name because I saw his face this week on

---

[19] This column was written in June 2009, the week after a white supremacist shot and killed a guard at the Holocaust Museum in Washington, DC. The elderly shooter died in custody while awaiting trial.

MSNBC. He was the officer killed at the same forward post he held on the day of our visit.

There are so many issues I'd like to raise with this story and so little space.

Take your kids to this museum, because Mr. Johns' death reminds us in no uncertain terms why such a trip is necessary. Take them soon, if only to peacefully protest his death. While my kid is a museum addict and thus not a valid measure of its broad appeal, I can safely say that I've never seen a bored teenager in attendance there.

Talk with your kids about the meaning and impact of racism, intolerance, and social injustice, not just as it has impacted our society historically, but as it impacts us today. It's easy to write-off this 88-year-old shooter as some kind of an isolated nutcase. But he was in fact a longtime purveyor of hatred. Our best defense against this kind of thinking will never be legal statutes, wars, the surrender of our civil rights, or mindless panic. Instead, the Good Book tells us that, "Wisdom is protection just as money is protection, but the advantage of knowledge is that wisdom preserves the lives of its possessors" (Ecclesiastes 7:12). Amen.

Let's educate our children about the roots of extremism in all its forms, and teach them to stand tall against oppression. It shouldn't just be our soldiers or law enforcement officers who bravely oppose those forces, but all of us alongside them to deny the terrorists their terror.

Recently, we've seen several such acts of violence, none of which had anything to do with far away countries, foreign political movements, or "Islamofacism" (whatever that is). These events happened in Wichita and DC, in Little Rock and Blacksburg. As we pause to mourn the dead, let's be especially thankful for that vast majority of humanity who are humane and spend each and every day teaching our children to stay always among their ranks.

Kelly Kelin: Socially, our culture has been deemed the melting pot of the western hemisphere. Yet, in all its diversity there still remain those who wish to degrade others, especially through their own selfish demeanor, not fully aware of how it may truly impact the people around them.

It's hard to think that in today's society we're still struggling between the good and evil of what life has to offer. Some, who are unsatisfied with the status quo, decide to take matters into their own hands, leaving

behind bloodshed and tears. Those who commit heinous and unimagi
nable crimes leave our society with unanswered questions, forcing us to
seek our own conclusions.

As much as parents may attempt to shelter their children from the
outside world, chaos seeps through the cracks of our schools, churches,
and even museums. Yet, through these tragedies we can gain acknowl-
edgment and insight. As Wes noted, it's important to expose kids to the
intolerance that society still faces and help them find their own answers.

We must inform them of the troubles that may lie ahead, while reminding them that there are still a lot of good things life has to offer.
Blooming among our society are new doctors, lawyers, and teachers.
People still care for each other and show one another courage and
compassion. As you raise your children, share these same values and
show them the positive things of life—love, kindness, and honesty—as
a hedge against the bad.

Wes's story reminds me of the Greek tale of Pandora. Pandora was
given a sealed box full of all the evils of mankind. Her unfortunate
curiosity led her to open the box, unleashing its sinful power.

Yet, within the box remained one thing: Hope.

Highway to Hell

Dear Dr. Wes and Kelly,

I am a retired teacher, social worker, and CASA[20]. I've spent a half-
century evolving my spiritual beliefs after studying most of them to
some extent. I was raised Protestant, but it is my strong belief that
teaching children that there is a Hell—and that they might go to it—is
emotionally abusive and intellectually irresponsible. This is not a
popular view here in the Bible Belt, just north of the Dallas/Fort Worth
Metroplex. What are your views on this subject?

Dr. Wes: I got my start working with kids in United Methodist
youth ministry, where my father had served for over forty years. So I
was tagging along on high school youth camps while still in grade
school in the late 1960s and early 70s. Many of those groovy teens were

---

[20] Court Appointed Special Advocates are court appointed volunteers who help
convey the needs of foster children to the court.

dead center in the good, bad, and ugly of that decade. Even as a child, I noticed my father meeting them as they were and accepting them with an unconditional love that forms the foundation of the New Testament. At no point do I recall him mentioning Hell as a central theme in his outreach to teenagers.

For me, your question is less about theology than it is about methods of successfully engaging and communicating with teenagers. Kids are pretty savvy consumers of information, capable of turning off good messages presented in a way they consider demeaning or derogatory. Whether the threat of Hell is abusive or irresponsible I'm not here to judge, but I can tell you it's not a particularly effective way to convey the richness of several thousand years of religious thought and tradition.

Your question comes at a particularly interesting moment in our culture. Some believe that religious extremism—and I'll let you decide exactly what that term includes—has reached its worldwide zenith, creating a backlash where some folks claim that there's *nothing* good about religion; that faith is at the root of all of humanity's problems. I find that a sad and daunting perspective, especially because I grew up witnessing firsthand the value of the kind of spiritual journey you describe. I understand the critics, but I personally hope that the best aspects of

In a perfect world, we would live without conflicts over faith. Until we get there, we must try to do our best to resolve them in order to keep peace between each other.

religion, spirituality, and theology will win out in the end. And for my money, an emphasis on Hell won't draw many young people in that direction and will instead simply feed the backlash.

In 1990, over 400 people came to my dad's funeral, including a lot of former kids and families from those youth groups, many of whom travelled from all over the country to pay their respects. Some had even gone into ministry. Eulogizing my father before a standing-room only congregation, I realized just how successful he'd been in reaching out to young people with a simple message of grace.

Kelly Kelin: Although I'm agnostic, I find religion particularly interesting. I don't believe that in my eighteen years of living that I'm ready to choose and follow a religion. I haven't experienced enough yet. I also find that a lot of the religions I have looked into are very male-dominated, which I dislike.

I do see some very positive points in having a religious faith, including a strong identity, a sense of being, guidance on values and morals, and a perspective on right and wrong. Religion provides a secure foundation for those who want to know what might exist beyond this world. Yet, it depends on one's perspective. Some may look at one religion with delight, while others are shocked at what they see and hear of it.

Fortunately, we're all entitled to our opinions and to worship freely. These rights have been embedded within our Constitution and echoed throughout our history. Once you take away someone's right to worship however or whomever they please, you're taking away something so powerful and strong that people may lose their foundation and sense of being.

A few religions go against the grain of what we generally perceive as right. When is it okay to put a foot down and oppose these beliefs? What gives us the power to choose for others what they can and cannot believe? You may not agree with or respect what is being preached, but neither can you stop it. It is their faith and they can choose what to teach to their congregation. Unless the religious group physically threatens or harms someone, there isn't much you can do.

In a perfect world, we would live without conflicts over faith. Until we get there, we must try to do our best to resolve them in order to keep peace between each other.

Falling Down on Ethics

Dr. Wes: This column tries to balance parental and teen anxiety with a rational picture of the world, at times asking readers to reconsider what is worth worrying about versus the babel of media hype.

Within that context, I'll tell you what's really making me anxious right now. Teenage ethics. I'm genuinely worried that an increasing number of teens do not view life through any ethical framework. Webster's dictionary defines ethics as *"the study of what is good and bad; what is our moral duty and obligation both as individuals and as a society; and the values we hold personally, in our families and in our culture."* Of course it's better to act ethically than to be able to define it, but when it comes to ethical thinking and behavior, I fear we're losing a big chunk of the next generation.

I'm astonished at the increasing number of accounts I hear of kids stealing. They steal from shops downtown, some of which have actually gone out of business for inventory losses. They especially like to steal from Wal-Mart, justifying this as a sort of political protest against large impersonal corporations. They steal from their parents. They even steal from each other. I did a little investigation and found that I'm not the only one who is shocked. Juvenile officers with whom I've spoken have seen an alarming increase in first-time offenders, and these are just the kids who get caught.

Both at the high school and college level, young people report that the work is getting harder and the demands greater. In response, cheating is on the rise. Just Google the word and you'll find multiple news reports. There's also a distinct lack of ethics in personal relationships: bullying, dumping a friend to improve one's social status, spreading false rumors or embarrassing photos over the Internet, and unrepentant infidelity to romantic partners. And lest you think these are just the "bad seeds," I can assure you that they represent a cross-section of society, including many kids you'd never suspect.

Ethical reasoning is nothing less than the basic foundation of all human interplay. Every choice we make—as parents, teenagers, teachers, politicians, therapists, bloggers, etc.—is an extension of what we believe is good in the world. If we are violent, we are expressing the belief that violence is an acceptable way of resolving conflict, or that the person receiving it deserves to be harmed. If we give our time or money to the needy, we are expressing the value of beneficence. If we teach or serve in the military or the Peace Corps, we are expressing the position that we are serving the greater good, even if we are not paid well for it. How we assert these values impacts others.

When we make a decision for ourselves, we make a decision for everyone.

We could write thirty-five columns on why ethical conduct is threatened. It could be culture, music, divorce, lax discipline, cynicism, or an unhealthy dose of poor adult conduct, all of which desensitizes teens to the impact of their own behavior. For example, I am astonished at how many parents cheat on their child's other parent and then hold their children to a rigid set of dating rules. Care to guess how well that turns out?

When our ethics deteriorate, we lose our faith and trust in others, and when that goes, we tear apart the fragile fabric of our social contract with each other. That's not the sort of world we want our children to inherit.

Julia Davidson: I'll be frank. Ethics, morals, and all other decisions forcing me to stick to one and only one conviction scare the crap out of me. I'm only decisive if it's an urgent situation and even then I don't feel sure of myself. That isn't to say I don't consider myself an ethical person. I recycle. I don't push people down flights of stairs and laugh. Really, the word "ethics" hasn't meant diddly-squat to me. It seems like such a vague idea. Yet, I'm realizing its applications are countless and worthwhile.

I know teens today really are different about their ethics. It's puzzling when a fifteen-year-old can stand up for her beliefs against all others, then turn around and get crazy drunk a night later. At times, it seems as if the ethical stance that teens are taking is based more on societal opinions and less on their personal values or reasoning.

I'm surprised when I see my peers feeling obligated to have convictions and opinions to stick to, but acting so nonchalant about their personal values. It would be a lot safer to start a teen off with a good set of values and morals before tackling larger societal ethics. Only after you've solidified your values should you explore other beliefs, and I emphasize explore. Adolescence is the prime time to consider culture, media, society, friends, family, and yourself and make thoughtful decisions on your ethics. Don't be surprised to see your opinions change with what you learn, but never let your ethics be based only on someone else's. Consider as many options as you can before making your own decision.

Think of ethics as an all-encompassing way of examining what decisions you make and why. It's most important to have the "why" (personal values) before the "what" (personal decisions and opinions), but neither should be immediately answerable, or else you aren't thinking hard enough.

Stirring Empathy

Dr. Wes: Over the last twenty years, there's been an increasing concern in the literature regarding the development of empathy, or the lack thereof, among adolescents. This research approaches the issue from a variety of angles—sociological, neurological, and psychological—often addressing the exposure of teens to mass media.

Originally, this focused mostly on violent television and movies. Then, as video games and the Internet began to compete for leisure time, and cell phones interconnected everyone, the focus shifted toward those media as the culprit of underdeveloped empathy. Now, we have online bullying, and anyone's fifteen seconds of poor judgment or bad luck can run around the globe as a source of amusement a million times a week, forever. Anonymous and uncivil online free speech is now the norm, something the forefathers never could have imagined. None of this teaches our kids empathy.

So, it was a nice diversion last week when I took my kids to the *Coterie Theater*[21] at Crown Center in Kansas City on a day off from school. Waiting for the show to start, we found ourselves surrounded by a full house of junior and senior high school students on a fieldtrip, laughing and talking with a deafening exuberance.

Then the lights dimmed and the crowd quieted under the watchful eyes of teachers. The second of three short plays was *Flowers for Algernon*. As a teen, I read the short story, and later, the novel, so I knew what I was getting us into. Charlie, a mentally handicapped man, undergoes surgery to triple his IQ to 180. But after a few months, the procedure reverses and he slowly loses all the intellect he has attained. His decline is devastating to watch onstage and the actor who portrayed Charlie brought depth and meaning to every line.

> *Once we decide to empathize, our next thought must be, "What do I do now?" Too many of us are content to just empathize and hope the world will change itself.*

The stage at the Coterie is a semi-arena and we were on the front row, stage left. It was just the right spot to watch half the students react to the play. Football-player-sized boys brushed tears in the dark as Charlie desperately struggled with his plight. Girls sat, eyes wide and mouths open, imagining, I supposed, what it would be like to lose something so precious as knowledge. The entire room exploded into

---

[21] www.coterietheatre.org

applause at the end. It was obvious to this trained eye that the kids were deeply moved.

It occurred to me that whatever these teens did in their spare time, in that moment, connecting with this character, they felt a deep sense of compassion. They felt what it was like to be Charlie and perhaps found something of themselves in him, even as his predicament was so different from theirs.

And that, Dear Readers, is the definition of empathy.

I went home that day greatly encouraged, certain that some fieldtrips are better than others.

Ben Markley: I don't think human beings ever lose their capacity for empathy, whatever their age. It's too deeply engrained into our being. When I see someone trip and fall, I think "Ouch." If I see a little kid crying, my first thought is "Sad." I've cried, I've fallen, and therefore, I can relate.

If I react differently, it's because my brain tells me, "That person doesn't deserve my empathy." If the person who fell tripped me before, I'm less inclined to feel bad for him. Apart from these exceptions, empathy is a natural reaction, so the only way to lose it is to treat everything as an exception. That's what people are afraid of. Few are concerned about our lack of empathy for the exceptionally wealthy or criminals. It's when our exceptions start to include the less fortunate, the innocent, and the oppressed that eyebrows should be raised.

I do think our list of exceptions is getting longer. Look at the numerous sites that publish videos, pictures, and stories solely to embarrass people we will never know in real life. It's common recreation for my age group to sit around and laugh at people humiliated on YouTube for a mistake made while on the shooting end of a video camera. I shudder to think how famous I'd become if someone filmed my slip-ups.

Still, I'm not worried that empathy will be lost.

My concern is more subtle. Once we decide to empathize, our next thought must be, "What do I do now?" Too many of us are content to just empathize and hope the world will change itself. When we look back at the genocides of the twentieth century, we think, "Why didn't people stop this from happening?" Yet, I'm shocked by how easily I can change the channel to avoid violence and oppression in the news. As long as I keep a comfortable distance, I can feel secure in ignoring it.

This may be partially to the credit of almighty Facebook, where we can "support a cause" simply by clicking a button and never think about it again. I'm not as concerned about why we feel less empathy. It doesn't matter whether the fire was started by a faulty stove or an arsonist. Either way, we must put it out. So, my advice is to take this advice personally. It's easy to get lost in the crowd of your generation, but waking up everyone to a position of empathy and action begins by waking up yourself.

12 INTO THE FUTURE

I'm Movin' Out

Dr. Wes: It's an easy cliché to pick a point in a child's life and say, "There's no moment more important than this one." Yet, among the top contenders is when a newly minted adult leaves home for college, trade school, or the world of work. Facing the inevitable sense of grief and loss, we forget our most important parenting goal—keeping them from moving home again. Of course, most will come back at some point, whether just for the summer, after the breakup of a marriage, or in response to unemployment or economic downturn, but the ultimate goal of independence remains.

Teach kids that when you make a decision for yourself you make a decision for everyone.

The best thing you can do to make this transition as successful as possible is by balancing support with good boundaries. There are more guidelines for this than we have space to print, but here's a few that should help in the process:

Don't give up on the dorms for the first year. None of us really liked them, but dorms are the place to meet people, sleep, and get food, the three most important elements of transitioning out. Greek houses are another alternative, but of course the student will still end up in the dorms the first year.

Be a careful consumer of apartments. If there are no dorms for your student, or if she's entering the work force, be very cautious about the move to an apartment. Any decent complex requires a co-signer. Understand that this means you're signing on to be liable for any debts incurred in that apartment by your child and all roommates. You'd better be ready to carry it 100% on your own for several months if things go south, and there are more ways for that to happen than you think. Even if your child is very conscientious, anyone's fortunes in school or work may turn. Expect the best and plan for the worst.

Coach children kindly but tenaciously on finance. After the age of eighteen, you can't control whether your child gets a credit card or checking account, but you should try and discourage both. Credit cards for young adults are little more than an invitation to self-ruin. Checking accounts might seem safer in comparison, but one $4.56 latte can cost ten times that much in overdraft charges before your child even realizes that his subtraction isn't all it's cracked up to be. Debit cards are even more dangerous. Some parents offer overdraft protection. I wouldn't do it. Until your child can afford that service, stick with a prepaid cash card until your child can save up enough to safely back a checking account. The card's extra fee will be worth it in the long run.

Teach kids that when you make a decision for yourself you make a decision for everyone. Young adults may pretend they are independent islands in the flowing stream of life, but none of us are really all that free. When they need to be bailed out of jail, homelessness, financial ruin, school failure, early pregnancy, or bad relationships, guess where they'll turn? Parents must set clear boundaries, but in the end it's hard not to ask for help when we need it and it's hard for parents not to give it.

Kelly Kelin: My graduating class and I will be moving on to adulthood soon. With this transition comes the good, the bad, and the ugly. This includes whether or not you decide to move out and take on the responsibility of independent living. Many of us have been ready to take that step since we entered high school. Parents may agree or disagree with our actions, but in the end realize that this is our time to prove ourselves; to show our parents that after all their hard work we are ready to advance.

If you're going to be living on your own, be sensible about it. Don't get caught up in the whole college party scene. Remember, the point of going is to get an education, not to see how many beer bongs hits you can do. Running around completely wasted all the time does not show much responsibility, and if you attempt to continue with this lifestyle, chances are you'll probably end up back at home, living with your parents.

Another adult responsibility is paying bills. If you rent an apartment or house, the bills will be somewhat higher than expected. To avoid debt, start saving money now. Get a job and don't waste your paychecks on unnecessary things. Be practical. If the rent is due, that $4.56 vanilla latte you just drank looks a little wasteful. Make sacrifices and straighten out your priorities.

Parents may find it hard to let their children go through this process. There will be no more curfews, or checking in. But have faith in your child. You've raised them to the best of your abilities and now it is time for you to let go, and for them to begin living their own lives.

Not College Bound

Dear Dr. Wes and Samantha,

I am frustrated with my son. Now is the time to be submitting his college applications and he is telling me that he wants to lay out a year. We have a lot of this paid for because we have had 529 savings accounts since that law was created, but the rest he needs to earn in scholarships. I'm afraid he's wasting an opportunity. He says he'll be more ready to go in another year. I say he'll never go if he doesn't go now.

Dr. Wes: You're both right. Over the years I've really changed my thinking on this, as kids seem more inclined than ever to squander great opportunities for higher education. If your son says he's not ready to go to college, then maybe he knows himself better than you do. Maybe he's heading off a disaster before it happens.

I have a whole subspecialty working with young adults who should have laid out a year or two and gained some perspective and maturity. Instead, they wasted scarce resources on a college career spent drinking and flunking out. And I've also seen kids who did okay in school but ended up at twenty-two with a degree they didn't want or couldn't use because they lacked the vocational identity to plan for a career. Either way, precious savings or student loan monies went down the drain.

Typically, the problem involves putting too much distance between the young person and the bill. No parent should pay every dollar of college expense. If kids don't carry at least a small part of their expenses, they're less likely to value the educational purchase. Free things aren't usually taken as seriously as those we earn ourselves.

On the other hand, your son should give some serious thought to why he's doing this and what he's going to do instead of college. If his plan is to sit around your house, eat your food, play your Xbox and be underemployed, he should seek a little more guidance before blowing off college. One of the joys of getting an education is not having to be out in the "real world" quite so soon.

If he wants to work thirty or forty hours a week, live at home under reasonable young adult rules or move out into a cheap apartment, that might actually work for a couple of years. Just be sure not to stake him If you want him to spend your money on college, keep it in reserve and release it when he's ready. He can fund any other adventures he wishes to have in the meantime. Just be aware that it's easy to get "stuck" with a young adult who wishes to neither toil nor spin. Sam offers some good guidelines for avoiding that very situation below.

As for never going back, *nothing* is a greater motivation for attending college than a couple of years out in the world of work, trying to make ends meet. In this, what your son really needs to watch out for is self-deregulation. Without the structure of college, kids may drift into a lot of unfortunate things, a few of which are difficult to reverse. But as long as he avoids debt, legal problems, accidentally starting a family, and addiction, he should be plenty eager and able to get back to school when the time comes, which it probably will.

Samantha Schwartz: I can see why you're worried. You don't want the highlight of your son's daily learning to be the *Colbert Report*. However, if you want to maintain a relationship with him, you should at least listen to his perspective. In planning his next year, you need to discuss the following:

Work. What job would he like to hold in his year off? Have him meet and shadow someone who has his desired job. Help him brainstorm questions concerning paychecks, promotions, and hours. If he plans to do volunteer work, decide if you're financially able to support him, or if he needs to take a side job to make money.

Expenses. Does he plan to live at home? Set up a rent payment system. Look online for a reasonable rate in your area for a room and bathroom the size of his. Don't forget to add costs for food, laundry, and other expenses. Does he want to get an apartment in town? Don't pay the rent, or pay it only while he looks for a job. Help him move in and bring him a housewarming gift of his favorite food. But past moving day, your dwellings are separate. As a general rule, don't let him visit more than once per week. Don't do any of this in a hostile way, but as a learning experience.

Goals. What is his long-term plan? Find out how this time off fits into the greater plan for the rest of his life. Have him make a list of useful things he thinks he will get out of this break.

Have a backup plan ready. Have him apply to at least one school you think he's likely to get into. Tell him he does not have to go, but you don't want him to regret not applying anywhere when all of his friends get acceptance letters in April and are gearing up for college.

Hard to Say "Goodbye"

Dear Dr. Wes and Kelly,

I am a mom with a senior who is leaving for college in the fall and desperate for advice on how to handle this. I have been a stay-at-home mom, and after my child is gone, I don't know what I'm going to do with myself. I think that my child knows this, which is making the transition all the more difficult. My friends have kids leaving or that have already left and they seem to be just fine. I even think I'm starting to get depressed about it. Is this normal? I sure don't feel like it is, and every day brings graduation closer. I feel really guilty.

Kelly Kelin: One of the proudest moments in a parent's life is when they see the child they've raised to the best of their abilities reach an important milestone. For some, this brings tears of happiness and for others tears of sadness. But in these defining moments, we realize that throughout our journey we have stuck by each other through thick and thin.

As you watch your children grow into wonderful, capable adults, it's hard to realize that they will soon be leaving home, which may create many problems. But you will not be the only one suffering from emotional detachments. Your child will also bear the brunt of these mixed feelings.

Of course, it's only natural for you to worry about your son or daughter. The world can be a challenging place, especially right now, and it will test every value you've raised them to uphold. You've sculpted them into young adults. Yes, they'll do things that may disappoint you, but continue to show your support and encouragement as they strike out on their own. Show faith and confidence in your child.

Just because you can't physically be with him or her, doesn't mean your child won't carry a piece of you everywhere they go. And there are other forms of communication—such as email, texting, phone calls, and snail mail—that can tide you over until you get together again. You can come to visit; just remember not to be too overbearing. It's time for your child to embark on a new journey, and no matter where it leads, your teen will always know he or she has a place in your heart called home.

A major obstacle is not your child's dependency on you for emotional support, but your dependency on him or her. That's not a wise or fair place for your child to be at this point.

Dr. Wes: Don't worry. Most young adults are not fully detached from their families until their mid-twenties, so you have plenty of time left. And, if you do the transition right, you'll find the next few years just as fulfilling as those from zero to eighteen.

From your letter it seems that a major obstacle is not your child's dependency on you for emotional support, but your dependency on him or her. That's not a wise or fair place for your child to be at this point. He or she probably does sense your anxiety and grief and may well respond by either cutting you off to avoid the trauma, or giving in and sticking around to support you. If either of these rings true in your case, then spend a lot of time *right now* getting out in the community to do volunteer work, picking up a part-time job, playing poker, or any other activity that puts you back in touch with your non-parent side. If you're still married, take this time to reignite the flame and focus more attention on your spouse. If you're having any problems in that realm, you might want to throw even more energy and perhaps some marital counseling into the mix. And consider some counseling for yourself to help get you through the process of separation.

If you have a support system in place, then your child will feel more relaxed about leaving home and can stay focused on the road ahead. After all these good years, you want to be sure you give your child the kind of send-off that will increase the chances of a successful young adult life. Both of you deserve it.

Sense of Absence

Dr. Wes: It is mid-August. Summer is in its slow and hot ebb. September is close, but not close enough. When it arrives, it will begin a transition of seasons toward renewal as the heat withdraws, the rains hopefully return, the grass turns green and the grain yellows. It will also bring the season of loss for those who have a teenage family member or friend leaving for college. Some will relocate to schools far from home. Others will be just across town. It really doesn't matter much, since the distance created by a child's leaving home is not measured in miles. It is measured in the heartfelt sense of absence that begins around age thirteen and now culminates in packed bags and hauntingly empty rooms.

I am feeling that loss too this week, as Marissa Ballard leaves Double Take for Pittsburg State University in a few days. Marissa was involved with the column from the beginning and has really left her mark as its co-author over the last year. To say she will be missed both personally and professionally is an understatement. As I turn this final column over to her to share her closing thoughts, I want to remind all those grieving of a simple truth that is often forgotten during these waning days of August: The point of raising kids is to let them go.

Parenting is one of the rare professions in which we are fired by our best customers. It's only when we are most successful that we get to feel the pain of loss because we have fulfilled our duty to our children. Transitioning out of the home is bidding farewell to one relationship in order to make space for another. If those rooms seem empty next week, remember that they will one day be filled with guests—young adults who come home with their loved ones and, later, their own children. As such, this season of goodbye should be embraced along with the other gifts of September, when we are reminded that before anything can grow, something else must pass.

I wish Marissa the very best on the road ahead, and expect to get an email from her now and then.

Marissa Ballard: My last column. Those three small words conjure up a flurry of emotions. I am happy, devastated, ecstatic, nervous and, all-in-all, content. I feel that I have done a decent job this year and I am leaving Double Take with confidence.

When Wes first told me of his and Jenny's idea for this column, I thought of it as a sort of "Dear Anne" aimed at teens and parents. It was an incredible idea for how we could convey important information to families in a unique and fresh way, and I was honored to be a part of its creation. I believe we've helped at least a few people throughout this year, although I was sometimes challenged by the questions we received. There were times I wished a sentence or two would have sufficed.

I can't list the many different ways I've changed and grown while writing this column, but the way in which it's helped me form strong opinions has been extremely beneficial. You can't share your point of view on a topic when you don't exactly know how you feel about it; especially when there's the possibility of thousands of strangers reading those opinions. Writing has forced me to become an independent and outspoken young woman, which is an invaluable characteristic.

I want to thank everyone who has read my work. I have had people approach me as if they already know me and discuss how they felt about the week's topic. That was amazing, and I know that I would not have met some of the people I have without Double Take. I must also thank my parents for their support even when they disagreed with my advice, and Wes for his patience, and for treating an eighteen-year-old with a year or so of journalism experience, as an equal.

Being There

Dr. Wes: It's been two years since we graduated a senior from the Double Take column, so this year we graduate two. Last year's co-author Julia Davidson, who'll be leaving shortly for Macalester College in St. Paul, Minnesota, and this year's author, Kelly Kelin, who is headed down the street to wear the crimson and blue, and wave the wheat at The University of Kansas.

In the coming days, throughout our community and across the country, parents will be packing up their children and sending them out into the world. Many will leave for college or trade school, others for the workforce. All will go with a mixture of excitement, loss, and trepidation. This year's transition is made more poignant by the consistent uncertainty we feel as our country undergoes many transitions of its own—some wondrous, many worrisome. It's hard enough to launch our children into the calm seas of economic prosperity. It's excruciating to do so during an economic downturn.

A cause for hope lies no further than our history books—those dry tomes that kids leave behind in high school and find again in college. These tumultuous times may try our souls, but they are far kinder to our children than any other in history. Despite previous adversities, the next generation has always found a way. Our wars are small compared to the World Wars; our economic deprivation mild compared to the horrors of the Great Depression. Our safety has never been greater. Of course, we hope for perfect peace and prosperity and to live in the healthiest environment, but today we would do well to send our kids off to the next phase of life with a sincere hope for personal growth and enlightenment, an intense desire to work hard for what they want, and a goal of advancing our best values and ideals. To do without and to make do is a greatly underrated talent that has become all too scarce.

Teens leave home with overdeveloped yearnings for freedom and underdeveloped skills of independence. However, they soon learn that freedom was the easy part and, as they increasingly struggle toward self-sufficiency, they grow in character and self-assurance. As we say goodbye to our children, let's welcome our new adults into the world and give them the best gift of all—the belief that they will find ways to unscrew what we've screwed up just as we did for our parents. History tells us that we were more successful than we may think and that our children will outdo us yet again.

An old professor of mine ended each semester with this benediction: "I don't know where you'll be someday, but I know you'll be there."

It makes more sense the more you think about it.

Kelly Kelin: So, this is it. My final curtain call to a short but sweet era of my life, which is only making me nostalgic. Throughout my experience at Double Take, I've not only learned a lot about human behavior and today's culture, but I've unexpectedly learned a lot about myself: the importance of compassion, consideration, and aptitude. In fact, I would have never expected to end up where I am today. I'm not exactly sure what my future has in store for me, but I know that when I look back, this will be one of the important milestones I passed, and one I will never forget.

When I first signed on for this job, I was skeptical of my ability to give advice to teens and parents. With my seventeen years of living I wondered how I could successfully put myself out there for the public to see. I thought no one except my parents would even take a glance at my insights.

I was proven wrong.

I was shocked to see how much praise I got from my peers, parents, teachers, and even complete strangers who recognized me around town. Knowing that, in some small way, I've left my footprint on this community and across the Internet means a lot to me.

I'm sad to see this opportunity go, but I know that with determination and a positive attitude I'll find plenty more like it coming my way. My advice for next year's columnist: You have some small shoes to fill.

Literally. I'm a size-7.

Masterpiece Self

Dr. Wes: August is upon us, the season of goodbye as our eighteen-year-old friends, neighbors, and children head off to college. Ben Markley will be headed down the highway to Johnson County Community College to begin an undergraduate degree in Philosophy with an eye toward transferring to The University of Kansas, and then on to seminary.

It always proves to be a long year when you're a teenage newspaper columnist. I warn everyone when they sign on that churning out fifty columns in twelve months can be a grind, yet Ben did it with aplomb. Scarcely a week goes by without someone commenting on how much they enjoy both his writing style and content. We'll miss him as we have every co-author over the years, grateful to have shared a wisp of their lives, as they pass through the door of adolescence and on to adulthood.

A whole lot has changed since we started this column in November 2004, when Ben would have been about eleven-years-old. We were embroiled in warfare, the memory of 9/11 still fresh in our minds. We thought Xanga was the latest thing. Texting was something you paid for by the message and many a family opened their monthly phone bill in horror to learn their teen went $228 over their limit. We used AIM a lot.

A young Harvard student got the jump on Double Take by about seven months in launching his own project, a little thing he called The Facebook. Over the years he's gotten ahead of us in audience share, but we're hoping to catch up soon.

What hasn't changed since then is the consistent quality of writing our area teens bring to this column and the astounding opportunity the Lawrence Journal World gives them by providing a barrel of ink each year to allow their voices to be heard.

Ben, we'll certainly miss yours.

I'm fully convinced that, just after Religious Leader, Advice Columnist might potentially be the most hypocritical job ever.

Ben Markley: This column taught me something pretty significant—that each person is really two people. Unlike Dr. Jekyll, who thought there was a Good and Bad Self, it's more accurate to say there's an Everyday Self and a Theoretical Self. The Theoretical Self, always does the right thing for the right reason, unfazed by circumstance or consequence, and he or she exists primarily in our imagination. Theoretical Self is the one Socrates was referring to when he said, "Be as you wish to seem."

I'm convinced my columns were written by Theoretical Ben because when I go back to read them, I'm amazed at how badly I needed my own advice. It's downright unsettling to see your name published just above your own good advice that has seen no shadow of application in your life. I'm fully convinced that, just after Religious Leader, Advice Columnist might potentially be the most hypocritical job ever. As I leave and ask myself what I'm going to do about Theoretical Ben, I'm reminded of Alexander Ivanov who spent twenty years of his life on one painting. While it never became the painting he had in his head, it was still a masterpiece.

People are like that. We may never become that perfect person we like to imagine, but we can still turn out to be pretty great people if we try. I don't know how long my painting is going to take, but I'm pretty sure I want it to be a masterpiece. That's my goal as I go into the adult world.

Thanks, everybody! This has been a blast.

ABOUT THE AUTHORS

Wes Crenshaw, PhD is a licensed psychologist and Board Certified in Couples and Family Psychology by the American Board of Professional Psychology. He specializes in working with adolescents and their families from his private practice in Lawrence, KS. He is the author of *Treating Families and Children in the Child Protective System* (Brunner-Routledge, 2004) and chapters several in other textbooks. He has co-authored Double Take since November 2004. Dr. Wes has been married since 1985 (to the same woman, no less) and has two children, including a teenager who helped him immensely in both the conceptualization and final editing of this book. He is presently working on another set of books based on Double Take, while finishing his novels. You can learn more about his writing and practice and submit your own question to Double Take at www.dr-wes.com or follow his advice for parents and teens on Twitter at @wescrenshawphd.

Jenny Kane (Co-author, 2004-2005) discovered her passion for journalism working on Double Take. After graduation from Free State High School she went to Western Kentucky University to pursue her dream of becoming a photojournalist. While in school she interned for the Topeka Capitol-Journal, The Oregonian, and the Monroe Evening News. In 2010 she graduated with degrees in Photojournalism (emphasis in multi-media) and Political Science. After graduation she spent a year at the Patriot-News as a post-graduate fellow. Currently she is working for the Northwest  Herald in Crystal Lake, Il as a video journalist. Follow her work at www.jennykane.com.

Marissa Ballard Hemenway (Co-author, 2005-2006) graduated with a BS in Education from Pittsburg State University. She married her junior high sweetheart, Arna Hemenway, in July of 2010 as described at the end of Chapter 2. In October of 2011, they welcomed a daughter, Bluma, making Marissa the first Double Take author to start her own countdown to parenting an adolescent. The Hemenways are currently living in Iowa, where we will forward a future edition of *Dear Dr. Wes...Real Life Advice For Parents of Teens* in exactly thirteen years.

John Murray (Co-author, 2006-2007) recently received his BA in Philosophy from The University of Kansas. He enjoys reading about rational choice theory and playing Settlers of Catan, hopefully in moderation as recommended in Chapter 8 of *Dear Dr. Wes: Real Life Advice for Teens*. His current projects include learning Python programming and teaching his little brother economics (photo by *Insight Photography*, Lawrence, KS).

Julia Davidson (Co-author, 2007-2008) is a second-semester junior at Macalester College in St. Paul, Minnesota. She is currently working on a combined major in Theater and Dance with a Critical Theory concentration. In her free time she goes on long walks and coffee dates with her friends. Julia future hopes and dreams include working in field of dance and bodywork, incorporating the caring and compassion rooted in the realm of therapy. Her present hopes and dreams are for the success of this book, the continuation of the Double Take column, and the best cup of coffee in town!

Kelly Kelin Woods (Co-author, 2008-2009) is an undergraduate at The University of Kansas. She is currently majoring in English and hopes one day to become a writer. After graduation she plans on traveling around the world to look for potential graduate school opportunities to further her career and life experience.

Samantha Schwartz (Co-author, 2009-2010) is a sophomore at Grinnell College in Iowa, majoring in psychology. If you've read her advice in this book, you'll know why. In fact, she currently works as a Wellness Coordinator at her college, working to make a difference in both the physical and mental health of other students. She plans to attend graduate school in 2014 to pursue a PhD in psychology, and hopes to focus once again on teen issues—about which she has proven her expertise time and again in the pages of this book (photo by *Insight Photography*, Lawrence, KS).

Ben Markley (Co-author, 2010-2011) graduated from Lawrence Free State High School in 2011 and is currently attending Johnson County Community College where he is studying creative writing and philosophy. He is considering seminary after he earns a bachelor's degree and hopes to pursue a writing career in the future. That won't surprise Double Take readers, given the number of comments we received during his year on both the quality and style of his work.

Miranda Davis (Co-author, 2011-present) is a senior at Lawrence Free State High School and co-editor-in-chief of the *Free State Free Press*. She admits that, as a freshman, she read Samantha Schwartz's advice every week and considered her "the most brilliant teenager ever." That apparently paid off, because three years later Miranda won her chance to be brilliant. After graduating in May, she plans to attend The University of Kansas to study journalism. Miranda showed special courage in serving her term on Double Take at the same time this book was being complied and sent to press, allowing her to put up with more than her share of "Dr. Wes Stress."

About Our Town

Lawrence, Kansas was burned and sacked and its citizens murdered before it was ten years old. Twice. Not surprisingly, its symbol is The Phoenix. Certain folks in Missouri didn't agree with our liberal views on slavery back in the 1850s and 60s, and we still have border clashes with them to this day. Fortunately those take place on the basketball and football fields now. In honor of our history one of our high schools, a credit union, and a famous brewery now go by the name Free State as an homage to that radical notion of freedom for all.

Lawrence remains a unique, progressive, and vibrant intellectual and artistic community. It is home to The University of Kansas, a school of 29,000 undergraduate and graduate students, and Haskell Indian Nations University, a four-year college of 1000 students from Native American tribes all over the United States.

Having lived here now for twenty-three years, Dr. Wes is convinced that few other towns would have embraced Double Take as has Lawrence. We are still a community that believes in doing things a little differently than everyone else, and we do so proudly.

11210176R00120

Made in the USA
Charleston, SC
07 February 2012